Benedict Arnold

Hero and Traitor

Leaders of the American Revolution

Benedict Arnold

Hero and Traitor

Liz Sonneborn

CHELSEA HOUSE
PUBLISHERS
A Haights Cross Communications Company ®
Philadelphia

CHELSEA HOUSE PUBLISHERS
VP, NEW PRODUCT DEVELOPMENT Sally Cheney
DIRECTOR OF PRODUCTION Kim Shinners
CREATIVE MANAGER Takeshi Takahashi
MANUFACTURING MANAGER Diann Grasse

Staff for Benedict Arnold
EXECUTIVE EDITOR Lee Marcott
EDITORIAL ASSISTANT Carla Greenberg
PRODUCTION EDITOR Bonnie Cohen
PHOTO EDITOR Sarah Bloom
COVER AND INTERIOR DESIGNER Keith Trego
LAYOUT 21st Century Publishing and Communications, Inc.

A Haights Cross Communications ✦ Company ®

www.chelseahouse.com

First Printing

9 8 7 6 5 4 3 2 1

Library of Congress Cataloging-in-Publication Data

Sonneborn, Liz.
    Benedict Arnold: hero and traitor/Liz Sonneborn.
       p. cm.—(Leaders of the American Revolution)
    Includes bibliographical references and index.
    ISBN 0-7910-8617-8 (hardcover)
    1. Arnold, Benedict, 1741–1801—Juvenile literature. 2. American loyalists—
Biography—Juvenile literature. 3. Generals—United States—Biography—Juvenile
literature. 4. United States. Continental Army—Biography—Juvenile literature.
5. United States—History—Revolution, 1775–1783—Juvenile literature. I. Title.
II. Series.
E278.A7S66 2006
973.3'82'092—dc22

                                                                    2005004823

Contents

The
Vulture

On a cold, clear night, a dark figure hid in the trees along the Hudson River. He waited and waited, scanning the water for a small rowboat. Finally he saw it, floating slowly and quietly, heading toward the shore. The man jumped on his horse and raced to meet it.

The time was about two o'clock in the morning on September 22, 1780. The man was Benedict Arnold. He was one of the most famous people in the 13 American states. Arnold was a major general in the Continental Army, serving under the command of George Washington, and renowned for his force of will, physical strength, and tremendous courage. He was perhaps the greatest battlefield general in the War for Independence, the conflict that had been raging since 1775 between the British government and its American colonies.

That night, Arnold was on a mission, but not for the Continental Army. Unknown to his fellow soldiers, he had turned traitor. For months, he had been spying for the British. Now, he was planning the final stage of a plot to end the war with a British victory. Arnold was secretly meeting a British officer to discuss an upcoming attack on the American stronghold of West Point in New York. As commander of the post, Arnold planned to hand West Point over to British troops. An American defeat there, he thought, might be enough to end the revolution once and for all.

Once the rowboat docked, a man wrapped in a long cloak trudged up the shore. Arnold recognized him as John André, a British officer. To Arnold's alarm, he saw that André was wearing a bright red British uniform under his overcoat. It was a dangerous thing to do. If anyone saw them, they might guess that Arnold was committing treason, a crime that would be punishable by death.

Arnold and André talked for hours. Arnold first wanted to discuss money. The British government had promised him a sizeable fortune if his plot succeeded. But Arnold wanted assurance that, if the plan failed, he would still receive a portion of the reward. André was not authorized to discuss the subject, so they began talking about the campaign against West Point. Arnold brought with him a small stack of papers, on which he had drawn pictures of the post and written a detailed analysis of where it was most vulnerable. He gave them to André to take back to General Henry Clinton, the commander-in-chief of the British army in America.

As dawn approached, André wanted to take the rowboat to the *Vulture,* a British ship docked nearby. But the oarsmen waiting in the boat said they were tired and refused to take him. Arnold suggested instead that he and André head to the town of Haverstraw. There was a house called the Belmont, where André could hide for the rest of the day while they figured out a way to get

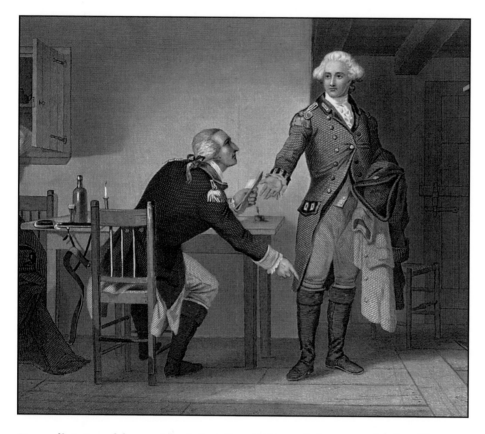

Benedict Arnold provided details of West Point to British officer John André, persuading him to hide the papers in the stockings concealed beneath his boots.

him back to the British ship after darkness fell. While they headed down the road toward Haverstraw, the men were stopped by a colonial patrol. Seeing General Arnold, the patrolmen immediately let them pass. Still, André was alarmed. For the first time, he realized he was behind enemy lines.

ANDRÉ'S ESCAPE

Once they reached the Belmont, Arnold ordered some breakfast and took André to a room upstairs to continue their conversation about West Point. As they spoke, a pounding noise shook the room. From the window, they saw a cloud of smoke rising above the river. American troops had fired upon the *Vulture*. Badly damaged, the ship had to pull out of American-controlled waters. André panicked as he watched the *Vulture* sail away. A British spy trapped in American territory, he was afraid for his very life.

Arnold, though, did not seem too concerned. He decided to leave for Robinson House, his headquarters near West Point. Arnold left André in the hands of his friend, Joshua Smith. Arnold wrote out two passes for André, one in case he was stopped on land, the other in case he was stopped on water. Instructing Smith to determine the best way to get André into British territory, Arnold rode off for Robinson House.

The next day, Smith stopped by to give Arnold a report. He assured him that everything was fine. Smith had given André an old cloak to better hide his uniform, and together they had traveled toward British-held territory. They were stopped several times by American soldiers, but they were promptly allowed to pass. Smith left André at a spot about 15 miles from a British outpost. Arnold guessed that André had already reached Clinton and delivered Arnold's documents safely into the hands of the British just as they were making their last-minute invasion plans. All Arnold had to do was wait for the British troops to arrive so he could hand West Point over to them.

A PLOT UNCOVERED

Two days passed. Arnold remained calm, not displaying a hint of nervousness that might make his aides suspicious. He even stayed completely composed when he received word that George Washington, Commander-in-Chief of the Continental Army, was on his way to Robinson House for a visit.

On the morning of September 25, the day Washington was expected, Arnold had a relaxed breakfast with his aides while his wife, Peggy, tended to their infant son, Edward, in a bedroom upstairs. Arnold's meal was interrupted by Colonel John Jameson, who brought him several dispatches. Arnold opened the first and read it carefully to himself. He betrayed no emotion, even though it contained disturbing news.

The Americans had caught André. Even worse, they had discovered the documents hidden in his stockings. The dispatch added that the papers had already been sent on to George Washington. Arnold knew that Washington would know in an instant what the documents meant: Arnold, Washington's trusted friend, was a traitor.

Calmly, Arnold excused himself. He walked up the stairs, entered Peggy's room, and clicked the door lock. As he told his horrified wife what had happened, an aide knocked on the door, reminding Arnold that Washington was due to arrive any minute. Suddenly, the door flew open and Arnold bolted down the stairs. He shouted to his confused aides that he had urgent business at West Point and promised to return within the hour. Arnold then jumped on his horse and rode away as fast as he could.

Arnold raced toward the river. There, he had a boat crew who routinely waited to take the major general wherever he needed to go. Whipping his horse, hoping to make it go even faster, Arnold kept looking over his shoulder, fearing that Washington and his men might already be following him.

Finally, he reached his boat. He told the oarsmen to row as quickly as they could downriver, promising

Benedict Arnold

His treachery discovered, Arnold raced toward the safety of the British ship *Vulture*.

them two gallons of rum if they did as he said. Arnold knew his only hope was to reach the *Vulture,* which he prayed was docked in Haverstraw Bay, some 20 miles to the south. His crew rowed frantically. All the while, Arnold kept expecting to see American ships coming to intercept his tiny boat, but the waters were empty. Finally, after about two hours, the boat rounded Verplanck's Point, allowing Arnold to get his first full view of Haverstraw Bay. There, to his infinite relief, was the *Vulture.*

Arnold tied a white handkerchief to his sword, waving it in the air to tell the *Vulture* that he was a friend of the British. He knew at that moment that he was safe, free from the threat of imprisonment and execution at the hands of the Americans. But there was something else he would never be free of, not during his lifetime or even after his death—a reputation as one of the greatest villains in all of American history.

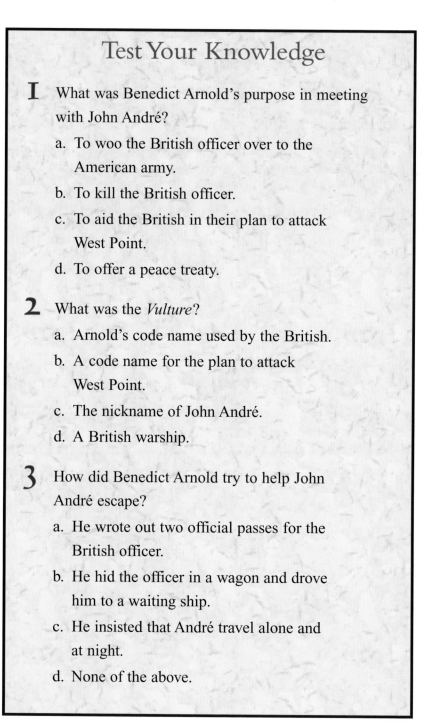

Test Your Knowledge

I What was Benedict Arnold's purpose in meeting with John André?

   a. To woo the British officer over to the American army.

   b. To kill the British officer.

   c. To aid the British in their plan to attack West Point.

   d. To offer a peace treaty.

2 What was the *Vulture*?

   a. Arnold's code name used by the British.

   b. A code name for the plan to attack West Point.

   c. The nickname of John André.

   d. A British warship.

3 How did Benedict Arnold try to help John André escape?

   a. He wrote out two official passes for the British officer.

   b. He hid the officer in a wagon and drove him to a waiting ship.

   c. He insisted that André travel alone and at night.

   d. None of the above.

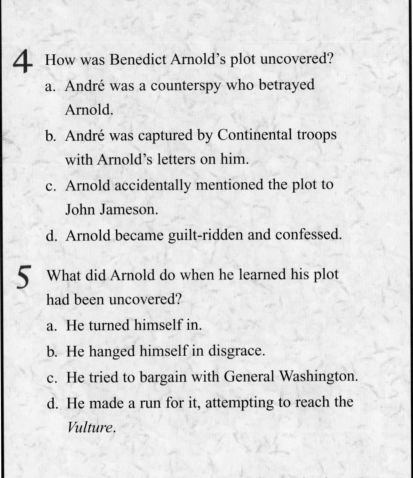

4 How was Benedict Arnold's plot uncovered?

   a. André was a counterspy who betrayed Arnold.

   b. André was captured by Continental troops with Arnold's letters on him.

   c. Arnold accidentally mentioned the plot to John Jameson.

   d. Arnold became guilt-ridden and confessed.

5 What did Arnold do when he learned his plot had been uncovered?

   a. He turned himself in.

   b. He hanged himself in disgrace.

   c. He tried to bargain with General Washington.

   d. He made a run for it, attempting to reach the *Vulture*.

ANSWERS: 1. c; 2. d; 3. a; 4. b; 5. d

Struggling for Recognition

On January 14, 1741, Hannah Arnold gave birth to a son. The boy was named Benedict, like his father. He was descended from a long line of colonial leaders. One ancestor had helped found Rhode Island. His son, also named Benedict Arnold, was elected governor of that colony ten times.

Benedict's father had left Rhode Island in the 1730s, and moved to Norwich, Connecticut. He had been a barrelmaker, but once in Connecticut he became a trader. Norwich was a lively commercial center. Goods from Canada, Europe, and the West Indies moved through the bustling coastal town. Benedict's father prospered in this trade and married Hannah King, a young widow from one of Norwich's oldest and most respected families. The Arnolds moved into a large house in a fashionable neighborhood where, after Benedict, they had four more children. All but his sister Hannah died young.

As a child, Benedict spent the cold Connecticut winters sledding and skating. In the warmer months, he went fishing and hunting, sometimes with boys from the nearby Mohegan Indian tribe. Benedict was high-spirited, a showoff who loved to play pranks. His mother, though, made sure he had the religious training befitting a young gentleman. Every Sunday, the Arnolds attended the town's Congressional church. They always sat in the first pew, a symbol of their high rank in Norwich society.

When Benedict was ten, his mother arranged for him to attend a private boarding school in

Benedict Arnold was born in Norwich, Connecticut, where
his family lived in this large home in one of the town's more
fashionable neighborhoods.

Canterbury, about 14 miles from his home. At the
time, only the wealthy could afford to give their
children formal schooling. The Canterbury school
was run by a minister who had graduated from Yale,
one of the oldest colleges in America. He instructed
Benedict and a handful of other students in history,

mathematics, classical languages, and the Bible. At the Canterbury school, Benedict was groomed to attend Yale and later to become a man of importance in the American colonies.

While Benedict was away, his mother wrote him often. He kept her letters for the rest of his life. Hannah Arnold told her son always to "watch over your thoughts, words and actions"[1] and urged him to "choose that your companions be your betters, that their good examples you may earn."[2] In 1743, Hannah also wrote Benedict about a terrible epidemic of yellow fever spreading through Norwich. The disease took the lives of two of his sisters, Mary and Elizabeth. Hannah did not want Benedict to return home because of the danger that he would catch the fever as well. Terrified that he would become sick, she urged him to prepare for death by praying and making peace with God.

Benedict survived the epidemic, but he was soon facing another crisis. His father was drinking heavily, and the family business was in financial trouble. As the Arnolds' fortunes faded, Hannah no longer had enough money to pay her son's tuition. Reluctant to leave Canterbury, Benedict came home to find his family in poverty and his father branded as the town drunk.

Humiliated, Benedict started misbehaving. Leading a gang of boys, he stole a few barrels of tar and set them on fire during Norwich's annual Thanksgiving celebration. The town constable and his men chased the boys. His friends ran away, but Benedict turned around, swinging his arms and threatening to fight the constable himself.

BECOMING AN APPRENTICE

Hannah decided something had to be done. She arranged for Benedict to live with two of her cousins, Daniel and Joshua Lathrop. They owned an apothecary, a shop that sold drugs and other goods. Benedict was to serve as the Lathrops' apprentice for seven years. As an apprentice, he would be their servant, forced to do anything his masters asked, until he was 21 years old.

In many ways, Benedict was lucky to be apprenticed to the Lathrops. While serving them, he lived in Daniel Lathrop's elegant house, one of the finest in all of Connecticut. Daniel's wife was very kind and treated Benedict and the other apprentices as her own children. Best of all, the Lathrops were eager to train Benedict in business. Clever and calm under pressure, he picked things up quickly. Not only did he learn how to run a shop, but he also took trading voyages to England and the West Indies to buy goods the Lathrops could sell.

Despite the Lathrops' generosity, Benedict ran away several times to join the militia. While he was an apprentice, the colonies were engulfed in the French and Indian War (1754–1763). The conflict pitted the British against the French and their Indian allies in North America. Militias, armies of colonists, were helping British troops fight the war. Finding shop-keeping a little boring, Benedict longed for the excitement of the battlefield, but his mother and the Lathrops kept bringing him back to Norwich before he could enter the fray.

In the spring of 1759, during one stint in the militia, Benedict learned that his mother was ill. He rushed home without leave, even though he could have been arrested as a deserter. His mother died, and his father began drinking more than ever, leading to his own death two years later. By the time he was 20 years old, Benedict was an orphan, forced to care for himself and his sister Hannah, his only surviving sibling.

IN NEW HAVEN

After he had served out his apprenticeship, Benedict Arnold wanted a fresh start. He and Hannah moved to New Haven, where he established his own shop with money lent to him by the Lathrops. New Haven was one of the largest towns in Connecticut and growing fast. Arnold's business expanded with it. His shop sold all kinds of goods, from books to tea. It was the only store in town that sold buttons, buckles, and jewelry— the type of luxury items Arnold himself loved to own. As the store grew, Arnold spent much of his time at sea, traveling on trading expeditions and leaving Hannah at home to run the shop.

By the mid-1760s, Arnold had become a prominent man in New Haven. Strong, handsome, and increasingly wealthy, he was also one of the town's most eligible bachelors. He courted and won the hand of Margaret Mansfield, the beautiful daughter of a prominent trader, with whom he eventually had three sons. Arnold's marriage to Mansfield helped further his rise in Connecticut society. But he also seemed to have had genuine affection for his wife. When they were together, he lavished her with gifts. And when he was away at sea, he wrote her frequently and lovingly, always begging her to send more letters.

Arnold began building a fine new house for his family. It was to be a symbol of his place in the community. With its grand staircase and wallpaper imported from England, it would tell all of New Haven that Arnold had a permanent place in the highest reaches of Connecticut society. But before the Arnolds could move in, his business was threatened with disaster. Suddenly, Arnold did not have enough money to finish building his showcase home.

CRISIS IN THE COLONIES

The French and Indian War had ended in 1763 with a British victory. But waging the war had been expensive. The British government decided that the colonies should help pay for the costs. It started levying taxes on the colonists and restricting their trade with anyone but the British. These trade restrictions made it almost impossible for colonial merchants like Benedict Arnold to make a living.

Britain's new trade policies made Arnold furious. For years, he had struggled to build his business and reputation, and now the actions of the British government could destroy it all. Arnold refused to stand by quietly. He wrote articles condemning the new laws in the *Connecticut Gazette.* He also joined the Sons of Liberty, a group dedicated to resisting the British policies, by force if necessary.

An American Smuggler

Many colonial merchants depended on trade with the Spanish, Dutch, and French islands of the West Indies. For decades, they shipped food, lumber, and livestock to these islands, where they traded them for sugar and molasses—goods that could be resold in the colonies for a healthy profit.

When Britain began enforcing laws that forbade this trade, many merchants faced bankruptcy. Some, including Benedict Arnold, decided there was only one thing to do. They became outlaws, illegally conducting trade in the West Indies as smugglers.

Smuggling was a difficult business. English warships roamed the waters off the coast of Colonial America. At any time, one might overtake a smuggler's ship, take its cargo, and even seize the ship itself. A trader could face both financial ruin and prison if he was caught smuggling goods.

One of Connecticut's most daring smugglers, Arnold had several run-ins with the authorities. The most notorious

By 1774, many other colonists were as disgusted with British policies as Arnold. Members of this resistance movement organized the Continental Congress, made up of representatives from each colony, to discuss their grievances with England. At the same time,

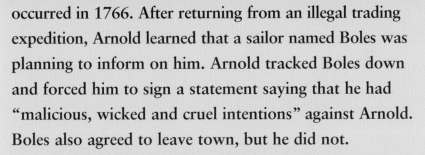

occurred in 1766. After returning from an illegal trading expedition, Arnold learned that a sailor named Boles was planning to inform on him. Arnold tracked Boles down and forced him to sign a statement saying that he had "malicious, wicked and cruel intentions" against Arnold. Boles also agreed to leave town, but he did not.

Arnold gathered a group of shipmates to help him communicate his displeasure in a more forceful way. His mob found Boles, tied him to a post, and whipped him almost to death. Arnold and his men then led the sailor out of town, promising an even worse punishment if he ever came back.

Arnold was placed on trial for the beating. Although he was found guilty and ordered to pay a small fine, many people in New Haven hailed him as a hero. They were tired of the British trade laws and appreciated Arnold's tough stance against them. Oddly, being a smuggler and a street brawler only enhanced Arnold's reputation among Connecticut's elite.

colonial citizens began organizing their own militias, in case the disagreement erupted in war. Arnold joined 64 other New Haven men in forming the Governor's Second Company of Foot Guards. The New Haven militia needed a captain to organize its military drills. A vote was taken, and Arnold was elected. Arnold was clearly intelligent and commanding. But perhaps even more important to his fellow militiamen, Arnold was always ready for a fight.

Test Your Knowledge

I What was Benedict Arnold's father's occupation?

   a. Admiral.

   b. Weaver.

   c. Barrelmaker and trader.

   d. Blacksmith and ironworker.

2 Which of the following best describes Benedict Arnold's childhood?

   a. Wealthy and privileged.

   b. Poor and hardworking.

   c. Sickly.

   d. None of the above.

3 What ended the Arnold family's prosperity?

   a. Yellow fever.

   b. A devastating fire.

   c. The Revolutionary War.

   d. Arnold's father's drinking.

4 Where was young Arnold apprenticed?

   a. With a barrelmaker.

   b. At a church.

   c. At an apothecary.

   d. With a shipwright.

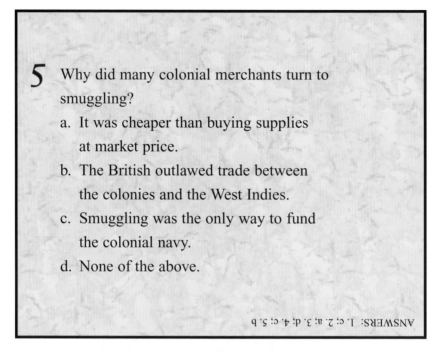

5 Why did many colonial merchants turn to smuggling?

a. It was cheaper than buying supplies at market price.

b. The British outlawed trade between the colonies and the West Indies.

c. Smuggling was the only way to fund the colonial navy.

d. None of the above.

ANSWERS: 1. c; 2. a; 3. d; 4. c; 5. b

OUR RIGHTS AND OUR LIBERTIES

Attack on Ticonderoga

W hile Arnold was training his militiamen, fighting broke out between American colonists and British troops in the colony of Massachusetts. The battles at the towns of Lexington and Concord marked the beginning of what would become known as the Revolutionary War.

While Arnold was training his militia, the battles at Lexington and Concord marked the start of the Revolutionary War, inspiring colonists with the stories of local militiamen forcing British Regulars to retreat.

Some Connecticut colonists were alarmed. But Arnold was thrilled. Here was his chance to march into war and earn recognition and respect. He immediately gathered together the men of his company. The following morning, they set out for Boston to help reinforce Massachusetts's militia.

Before Arnold reached Massachusetts, he ran into Samuel H. Parsons, a militia colonel who had just been in Boston. He told Arnold that the American troops there were in trouble. They did not have nearly enough cannons to fight the British.

Arnold got an idea. The year before, he had traveled to Canada on business. There, he passed by Ticonderoga, an old fort at the southern end of Lake Champlain. The fort was originally built by the French, but it was taken over by the British during the French and Indian War. For the past 20 years, the British had neglected Ticonderoga. It was now more a pile of ruins than a fort. But Arnold remembered that it still housed dozens of cannons. He decided that if he and his men could seize the cannons and bring them to Boston, he would be hailed as a hero.

A few days later, Arnold arrived in the town of Cambridge. There, he sought out Joseph Warren, the chairman of Massachusetts's Committee of Safety. Arnold persuaded Warren to back his plot to attack Fort Ticonderoga. With Warren's help, Arnold was made a colonel in the Massachusetts militia, with orders to recruit 400 men for his mission.

ETHAN ALLEN AND HIS BOYS

Unknown to Arnold, his idea was not new. Weeks

before, a lawyer named John Brown began campaigning for an attack on Ticonderoga. He even enlisted a ready-made army to execute his plan—the famed Green Mountain Boys led by Ethan Allen.

The Green Mountain Boys were a group of rough and unruly settlers from New Hampshire. They had

Powder House Day

On the morning of April 22, 1775, Benedict Arnold gathered the Governor's Second Company of Foot Guards on the village green in the center of New Haven. Hundreds of townspeople came to see the militiamen, who were about to march to Massachusetts to join the war. Reverend Jonathan Edwards said a prayer to bless their mission.

Arnold and his men were almost ready to leave. They only lacked one thing: gunpowder. Without it, their weapons would be worthless in battle. The town had a healthy supply. But unfortunately for Arnold, the town council held the key to the powderhouse. The councilmen were not sure that they supported the fight for independence, so they refused to open the powderhouse to Arnold's men.

Arnold marched his troops to a tavern to confront David Wooster, a 64-year-old man who was widely moved into lands west of the Green Mountains that were claimed by that colony. The British later decided that the land belonged to New York rather than New Hampshire, but the Green Mountain Boys refused to move. Instead, they waged a guerilla war against the New Yorkers who were trying to take over the area.

respected in New Haven. Speaking on behalf of the town fathers, Wooster tried to persuade Arnold that no one should take up arms against the British king. Arnold replied with a threat: If Wooster did not open the powderhouse, his men would break down the door. Wooster finally agreed to give Arnold the keys. Arnold's men raided the powderhouse and marched off, armed and ready for battle.

The confrontation between Arnold and Wooster is now a treasured part of New Haven's history. Every year since 1904, residents have celebrated Powder House Day on April 22. The focus of the holiday is a reenactment of Arnold's stand against the council, performed by current members of the Governor's Second Company of Foot Guards. The company members dress in bright red uniforms like those worn by Arnold's militiamen.

When the revolution broke out, the Green Mountain Boys temporarily gave up their cause to join the American rebels.

While Arnold was searching for recruits, he learned that Ethan Allen's men were already heading for Ticonderoga. Determined to take the fort himself, he raced off to New Hampshire. In a tavern in the town of Castleton, he found John Brown. Brown told Arnold that the Green Mountain Boys were planning their attack for the next morning.

Arnold was desperate to get in on the action. He insisted that he should command the men. After all, as a colonel, he outranked Allen. A scrappy fighter, Allen was not about to back down. In the end, both men agreed to share command.

A SNEAK ATTACK

Just after midnight, Arnold, Allen, and about 80 men climbed into a fleet of rowboats and paddled toward Ticonderoga. At dawn, they crept into the fort while the British soldiers stationed there were still asleep. As their men stormed the barracks, Arnold and Allen rushed up a staircase to confront the fort commander, Captain William Delaplace. By the time Delaplace

Benedict Arnold joined Ethan Allen in the attack on Fort Ticonderoga.

roused himself, the fort had been overrun by the Americans. He had no choice but to surrender.

Allen's Green Mountain Boys then went wild. To celebrate, they looted the fort and gulped down all the rum they could find. Allen was happy to have his men blow off a little steam. But Arnold was disgusted. He wanted the troops to make an inventory of the weapons they had seized and decide how to transport them to Boston. But all Allen's men wanted to do was get drunk.

On his own, Arnold began organizing the fort's supplies and making plans about what to do next. At the same time, he made his annoyance clear to anyone who would listen. Officers in the Massachusetts militia dismissed him as an arrogant blowhard. The Green Mountain Boys were even more irritated by his posturing. Some mumbled threats against Arnold, and a few even took pot shots at him.

STEALING THE SLOOP

Despite the opposition to his command, Arnold continued to plot his next maneuver. He was afraid the British were planning a counterattack on the fort. Arnold was especially concerned that the enemy had a sloop, a fast-moving ship, stationed at St. Jean on the north shore of Lake Champlain. If the British were planning to invade Ticonderoga, they would need this sloop to carry British soldiers and weapons. Arnold decided to destroy it.

With the help of 50 new recruits, Arnold set out for St. Jean on an American schooner. Once his scouts determined that there were few guards around the sloop, Arnold confronted the British there. Taken by surprise, they immediately surrendered. Arnold's men then loaded up the sloop, renamed the *Enterprise,* with British weapons and supplies and sailed away.

In the meantime, Allen had found out about Arnold's expedition. In four boats, he and about one hundred men headed out to stage their own attack on St. Jean. When Allen met Arnold in the middle of the lake, he mocked Arnold for not taking and occupying St. Jean. But Arnold knew that British reinforcements were likely to show up there any minute. Allen ignored his warning. Just as Arnold predicted, Allen and his men were chased away from St. Jean as soon as the fresh British troops arrived. Arnold's plan to steal the sloop also proved wise. Without the ship, the British gave up all plans to retake Ticonderoga, leaving the fort safely in American hands.

LEAVING TICONDEROGA

Hearing about the tensions between Arnold and Allen, Connecticut sent a three-man commission to investigate. The commissioners sided with Arnold. They wrote, "Had it not been for him everything here would have been in the utmost confusion and disorder."[3]

Any satisfaction Arnold took from their report did not last long. The Continental Congress ordered both Arnold and Allen to abandon Ticonderoga. Arnold was outraged. He wanted to launch an invasion of Canada from the fort. He sent letters to Congress outlining his plans. In his correspondence, he also angrily criticized Allen's leadership and shamelessly touted his own accomplishments.

Soon, Arnold was dealt an even harsher blow. Massachusetts surrendered control of the campaign to Connecticut, which decided to send a new commander to Lake Champlain. Arnold was furious at this decision. When the new commander arrived, Arnold refused to talk with him and left. After only a few months in the army, Benedict Arnold was ready to resign his commission.

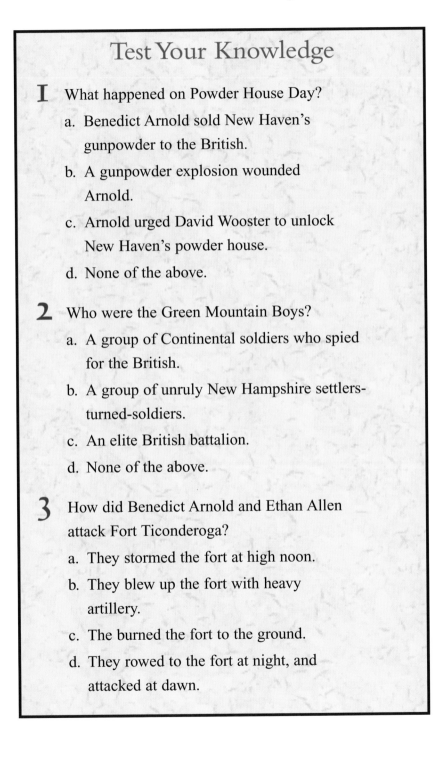

Test Your Knowledge

I What happened on Powder House Day?

   a. Benedict Arnold sold New Haven's
      gunpowder to the British.

   b. A gunpowder explosion wounded
      Arnold.

   c. Arnold urged David Wooster to unlock
      New Haven's powder house.

   d. None of the above.

2 Who were the Green Mountain Boys?

   a. A group of Continental soldiers who spied
      for the British.

   b. A group of unruly New Hampshire settlers-
      turned-soldiers.

   c. An elite British battalion.

   d. None of the above.

3 How did Benedict Arnold and Ethan Allen
     attack Fort Ticonderoga?

   a. They stormed the fort at high noon.

   b. They blew up the fort with heavy
      artillery.

   c. The burned the fort to the ground.

   d. They rowed to the fort at night, and
      attacked at dawn.

4 What did Arnold rename the captured
British sloop?

  a. *Intrepid*.

  b. *Endeavor*.

  c. *Invincible*.

  d. *Enterprise*.

5 What had Arnold planned to do after capturing
Fort Ticonderoga?

  a. Invade Canada.

  b. Ransom the fort back to the British.

  c. Build a city around the fort.

  d. None of the above.

ANSWERS: 1. c; 2. b; 3. d; 4. d; 5. a

Invading Canada

L eaving Lake Champlain, Benedict Arnold headed south, back to America. While traveling, he learned that his young wife, Margaret, had died suddenly. Arnold was inconsolable. He wrote Congressman Silas Deane that he felt his life was barely worth living.

Arnold realized that he had to keep busy if he were to survive his grief. As he told Deane, "an idle life under my present circumstances would be but a lingering death."[4] Despite his dissatisfactions with the Ticonderoga campaign, Arnold decided to immerse himself in military life. Leaving his sister to care for his children in New Haven, he took off for Albany, New York, to secure a new commission.

In Albany, Arnold hungrily sought an appointment as deputy adjunct general of the Continental Army. Hearing the stories about Arnold's inability to get along with other officers, Congress was slow to act. It also neglected to answer any of Arnold's letters about a campaign against Canada. He was still convinced that American troops should invade Canada before the British could send reinforcements there.

Frustrated, Arnold traveled to Cambridge, Massachusetts, to meet with George Washington, the Continental Army's commander-in-chief. There, he learned that Washington was also interested in a Canadian campaign. Washington envisioned a two-pronged attack. He wanted General Philip Schuyler to lead troops north along Lake Champlain to the city of Montreal. At the same time, another group of soldiers would travel up the Kennebec River toward the other major Canadian stronghold, Quebec.

Attacking Montreal and Quebec simultaneously would force British general Guy Carleton to make a difficult decision. He could split his troops between the two cities, but by spreading his army too thin he stood to lose both. Or he could decide to send his men to just one city, leaving the other defenseless. Either way, the Americans stood a good chance of scoring a substantial victory.

Arnold desperately wanted to lead the Kennebec expedition. Washington, though, was leery of Arnold's reputation. He also worried that Arnold did not have enough military experience to pull off the difficult mission. He would have to lead more than one thousand men through hundreds of miles of uncharted wilderness. In the end, Arnold's enthusiasm persuaded Washington to allow him to handle the mission.

A HARD JOURNEY

In mid-September 1775, Arnold's men set off by land for the Kennebec River. There, they boarded bateaux—long, flat-bottomed boats—to travel the river's rough waters north. Many men got seasick. Even so, most remained excited, with high hopes for their adventure. Arnold wrote Washington that he expected to reach Quebec in about three weeks.

But soon the men's optimism began to fade. Many of their bateaux were flimsy. They often leaked, soaking the men's food, supplies, and clothing. It rained heavily, chilling the tired soldiers. Food supplies were running low. Arnold began rationing what little they had and encouraged the men to hunt for moose and fish for trout. They soon reached the Dead

The Fourteenth Colony

When George Washington sent Benedict Arnold to Quebec, he gave him one very specific instruction. He insisted that Arnold make sure that his men treated all Canadian citizens with respect. There was a good reason for this order: Washington hoped that the Canadians could be persuaded to support the American cause. If so, all of Canada might join the revolution as the fourteenth American colony.

The idea was not farfetched. After all, Canada had been under British rule for only 16 years. (Before the end of the French and Indian War, Canada had been a colony of France.) Most Canadians did not have a strong sense

River, which scouts had promised would be easier to navigate. But the men found moving the boats against the river's strong current took every ounce of strength they had left.

Arnold could see that his men were growing weak and weary. He rallied them to draw upon their courage. He also conceived a plan to obtain desperately needed provisions. Arnold would ride ahead to the Chaudière River to buy food from French Canadians settled there. He ordered one of his officers, Roger Enos, to take a

of loyalty to the British. Many Americans assumed that the Canadians were as eager to win their independence from the British as they were.

Among them was Benedict Arnold. As he led his troops into Canada, he fully expected Canadian citizens to fight alongside his army. To his surprise, most Canadians were not interested in rebellion. In fact, many saw the invading American army as more of a threat to their lives and livelihoods than the British. Some people in Quebec did join the revolution, but not on the side of the rebels. They instead fought with the British to drive the American army from their city.

group of soldiers and gather up army provisions stored at Norridgewock Falls. Arnold's men were grateful that he was taking decisive action. They cheered as he left for the Chaudière.

When Arnold arrived at the French settlements there, he learned that Carleton had moved most of his British troops to Montreal, leaving Quebec relatively unguarded. Encouraged, Arnold purchased cattle and hundreds of pounds of flour. He sent these back to the detachments making their way to the Chaudière. But his men still needed the provisions Captain Enos was supposed to bring from Norridgewock. To Arnold's dismay, he soon found out that Enos and his men had abandoned their mission and headed home. Arnold's army now faced a long overland trek to Quebec with little food to sustain them.

Arnold led his men through the cold, dark wilderness. Many were sick. Others were barefoot. All were starving. To stave off their hunger, some even ate their pet dogs. When a few lucky soldiers came upon some cattle, they wept with joy. After slaughtering the animals, they were so hungry they could not wait to cook the beef and instead ripped it off the bones and swallowed it raw.

ENCOUNTERING THE ENEMY

Finally, the Americans made it to the St. Lawrence River. On the opposite shore stood Quebec. Arnold called together his officers. They had two choices. They could send their exhausted soldiers across the river to attack the city, or they could wait for the arrival of additional American troops, led by General Richard Montgomery, before taking action.

All of Arnold's officers wanted to wait. During their trip, hundreds of British soldiers had reached Quebec. They were armed and ready to fight. The officers didn't think the weakened American force could take them on. Arnold disagreed. He wanted to charge ahead with the original battle plans.

Arnold commanded his troops to head across the river in rowboats, traveling as quietly as possible. After the sun rose, Arnold lined his men up outside the city walls. He wanted to provoke Quebec's commander, Colonel Allan Maclean, to send his soldiers out to fight. Instead, Maclean's men lobbed a few cannon-balls at the American soldiers, forcing a retreat. Arnold's army set up camp and waited, enduring bitterly cold temperatures and raiding abandoned houses for food. Five days later, on November 19,

Arnold decided to withdraw, taking his men 25 miles west to wait for Montgomery's arrival.

AN ILL-FATED FIGHT

A few weeks later, Montgomery's 300 men straggled in. The Americans now could either attack Quebec or lay siege to the city, surrounding it so that no provisions could reach it. But the Americans did not have enough supplies to wait out a long siege. They also did not have soldiers and weaponry needed to ensure a successful attack. Having to choose between two bad options, Montgomery decided to attack during the next big snowstorm.

The Americans waited and waited. Their camps were cold and infested with insects. Many men fell ill with smallpox. Finally, on December 30, a blizzard began. Amidst snow and wind, the Americans rushed toward Quebec. From the beginning, they met heavy gunfire. Less than an hour into the battle, Arnold himself was struck. As a musket ball ripped through his calf, he fell down, bleeding in the snow. Two men grabbed him and carried him to a makeshift hospital.

Confined to bed, Arnold anxiously awaited news from the frontlines. When it came, it was not good.

The attack on Quebec proved costly. Arnold's men were forced to surrender, and General Richard Montgomery was killed in battle.

Montgomery had been killed, and his men had withdrawn. Arnold's men had been left to fight alone. Surrounded in the streets of Quebec, they were forced to surrender. Four hundred were taken captive by the British. The first major battle of Benedict Arnold's career had turned into a disaster.

Test Your Knowledge

I   What was Washington's plan for the invasion of Canada?

     a. A frontal assault against Montreal.

     b. A frontal assault against Quebec.

     c. A two-pronged attack against both Montreal and Quebec.

     d. None of the above.

2   What problem(s) confronted Arnold's troops on their journey to Quebec?

     a. Seasickness and leaky boats.

     b. Food shortages and starvation.

     c. Strong currents.

     d. All of the above.

3   Which of the following best characterizes Arnold's results at Quebec?

     a. It was a miserable defeat for his starving troops.

     b. It was a rousing victory that broke the British spirit.

     c. It was a protracted siege and an eventual draw.

     d. None of the above.

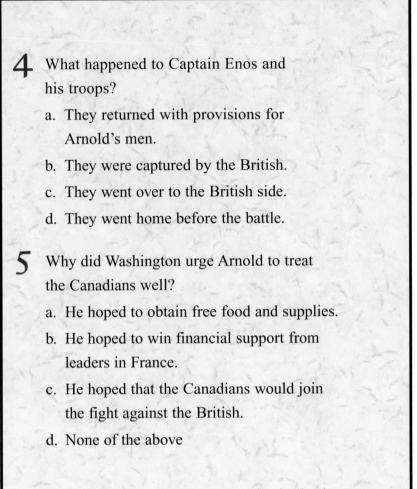

4 What happened to Captain Enos and
his troops?

   a. They returned with provisions for
Arnold's men.

   b. They were captured by the British.

   c. They went over to the British side.

   d. They went home before the battle.

5 Why did Washington urge Arnold to treat
the Canadians well?

   a. He hoped to obtain free food and supplies.

   b. He hoped to win financial support from
leaders in France.

   c. He hoped that the Canadians would join
the fight against the British.

   d. None of the above

ANSWERS: 1. c; 2. d; 3. a; 4. d; 5. c

On Land
and on Sea

Five days after the battle for Quebec, Arnold was well enough to leave the hospital. He found that his army was in miserable shape. The men were panicky and frightened, knowing they did not stand a chance if the British attacked their camps. Still in excruciating pain, Arnold tried to rally the troops and build their morale, all the while begging his superiors to send him fresh soldiers and supplies.

For his efforts, Congress promoted Arnold to brigadier general. He received little other support. Arnold longed to lead another campaign against Quebec, but without new troops it seemed hopeless. In April 1776, Daniel Wooster, a brigadier general Arnold knew from Connecticut, arrived to take command of the men. Arnold then headed for Montreal. There, he made a case for organizing an orderly withdrawal from Canada. He argued, "[T]here will be more honor in making a safe retreat than hazarding a battle against such superiority."[5]

But soon it was too late for Arnold's plan. On May 10, a fleet of British ships, full of soldiers, arrived at Quebec. The American army there responded by running away. With their haphazard retreat, any dream of the rebel Americans taking over Canada abruptly died.

COMMANDING A FLEET

The American military was facing an even greater problem. British troops led by General William Howe were preparing to attack the city of New York. If they could take New York, they would be poised to fight for control of the Hudson River Valley. This would be a nightmare for the American cause. The Hudson connected the northern and middle states. If the Americans could not transport goods and men along the river, they were doomed.

The only way to stop the invasion into New York was to keep British troops from reaching the city. Many were traveling south from Canada down Lake Champlain. The American strategy was clear: They would have to build a fleet that could stop the British troops. Even if the American fleet could not defeat the British on Lake Champlain, they might be able to delay them long enough to foil the British attack on New York.

Arnold had no experience commanding ships. Nevertheless, he was sure he was the right man to head the Lake Champlain campaign. Arnold persuaded the Continental Army to send him to the village of Crown Point to oversee the construction of the American fleet. In the meantime, American scouts tried to find out as much as possible about what the enemy was doing. They reported that the British were building a warship called the *Inflexible*. Arnold feared his small fleet would be no match for this heavily armed vessel.

With the odds stacked against him, Arnold positioned his ships in a small channel between the mainland and Valcour Island. Waiting for the British fleet, Arnold wrote to General Horatio Gates, "I hope to be excused . . . if with 500 men, half naked, I should not be able to beat the enemy with 7,000 men, well clothed, and a naval force, by the best accounts, near equal to ours."[6]

Two weeks passed. Finally on October 11, 1776, Arnold saw the British ships coming straight toward him, with the *Inflexible* in front. The two fleets battled for five hours before darkness fell. The American fleet was badly battered. Nearly every ship was damaged, and Arnold's men had used most of their ammunition. The British were confident that they could finish off the Americans in the morning. They would then sail south to recapture Ticonderoga.

That night, Arnold realized he had to make a daring escape. He commanded his ships to sail in single file down a mile-wide area of sea between the British ships and the mainland. While the British slept, the Americans quietly slipped away.

When the sun rose, the British realized that they had been tricked. Their fleet raced after the American ships. They caught up with one, the *Washington,* and forced its captain to surrender. Arnold's ship, the *Congress,* was more fortunate. It evaded the British vessels long enough to lead many of the smaller American ships into an inlet. Once the ships ran aground, Arnold ordered his men to set them on fire so that the British could not seize them. He and his men then fled overland, first to Crown Point, and then to Fort Ticonderoga.

The British ships were close behind the American fleet. General Gates frantically called for American reinforcements to protect the fort, though few arrived. For many days, Arnold and his men had nothing to do but wait for the British force to descend upon them. Finally, at the end of October, a few armed enemy vessels approached the fort. However, as soon as they were fired upon, they withdrew. The entire British force then headed north. General Carleton had decided that they did not have enough time to take Ticonderoga and establish winter camps before icy weather set in. For Arnold and the other American officers, Carleton's decision was a lucky break. At least for a few months, the Continental troops in the north would be safe from further attack.

After setting their ships on fire, Arnold and his men fled on foot, traveling first to Crown Point, and then to Ticonderoga.

A BATTLE IN CONNECTICUT

In late December 1776, Arnold was ordered to Rhode Island, where a fleet of British ships was spotted off the coast. While there, he learned that Congress had just promoted five officers to major general. He was not among them. Furious, Arnold wrote Washington that Congress's action was "a very civil way of requesting my resignation as unqualified for the office I hold."[7]

Making Enemies

Throughout his life, Benedict Arnold had an amazing ability to hold a grudge. In the early years of the revolution, this trait was on public display in his dealings with two subordinates: John Brown and Moses Hazen.

During the 1775 campaign at Fort Ticonderoga, Arnold became convinced that Brown was spreading rumors about him behind his back. The next year, Arnold retaliated. When Brown asked for a promised promotion, Arnold refused to give it to him. Brown then went to Congress to lodge a protest. Arnold responded by accusing Brown and another enemy, James Easton, of stealing baggage belonging to British officers. Brown said he was innocent and dared Arnold to bring his accusations to a public court. Arnold ignored the challenge, possibly because he had made up the whole thing.

Similarly, Arnold set out to destroy Hazen, who had once dared to second-guess his military strategy in Canada. In retaliation, Arnold claimed that Hazen stole army provisions and ordered his court-martial. In court,

Washington tried to soothe Arnold's hurt feelings and promised to lobby Congress on his behalf.

Arnold, however, headed to Philadelphia, Pennsylvania, to confront Congress himself. Along the

Hazen turned the tables on Arnold: He said Arnold was the one who had taken the goods. Arnold rose up, denounced the proceedings, and stormed out of the courtroom. The court acquitted Hazen and moved to arrest Arnold, but General Horatio Gates disbanded the court to head off any further embarrassment.

Brown and Hazen's war against Arnold was not over. In December 1776, both filed charges against him. Hazen accused him of defamation of character, while Brown charged him with a variety of crimes. Ultimately, an inquiry found Arnold guilty of Hazen's charges but it did not recommend any punishment. Brown's accusations proved more damaging, however. The following May, they were read before Congress. Armed with letters and other documents, Arnold refuted the charges, and Congress found he had done nothing wrong. But for the many congressmen who were already suspicious of Arnold, the entire affair only seemed to confirm that he was not worthy of their trust.

way, he stopped in New Haven to visit his family. At his house, a courier informed him that 2,000 British troops had landed on the Connecticut shore just 30 miles away. Arnold immediately rushed off to rally the militia.

With Daniel Wooster, Arnold gathered 600 men. They learned that the British had already invaded the town of Danbury and set it on fire. The British troops were headed toward Cedar Point, where they could board ships bound for New York. Rushing to stop them, the American force split in two. The group led by Wooster attacked the rear, while Arnold's men set up a barricade on the road to the coast to block the British advance.

They fought the British for hours, although they were greatly outnumbered. During the battle, Arnold's horse was shot and he fell to the ground. As he lay there, a British soldier rushed at him with a bayonet. At the last moment, Arnold was able to seize his pistol and shoot his attacker. Many of his men, however, panicked under the heavy fire. As they fled from the battle, the British reached their ships and sailed away.

Arnold's leadership in Connecticut finally earned him the rank of major general. But those promoted earlier still had seniority over him. He spoke before Congress to protest the situation and to ask to be repaid for military expenses he had paid out of his own pocket. Congress had no money to give him. Instead they presented him with a new horse, a gesture that did little to calm Arnold.

In disgust, he sent Congress a letter of resignation, but Washington urged him to reconsider. In July 1777, Ticonderoga fell to the British, who were now descending on the entire Hudson River Valley. In this time of crisis, Washington knew he needed Arnold to help fight the army's next, and possibly final, campaign.

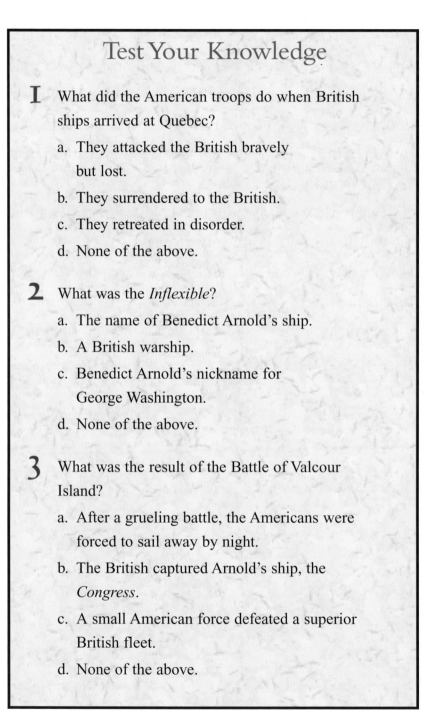

Test Your Knowledge

I What did the American troops do when British ships arrived at Quebec?

   a. They attacked the British bravely but lost.

   b. They surrendered to the British.

   c. They retreated in disorder.

   d. None of the above.

2 What was the *Inflexible*?

   a. The name of Benedict Arnold's ship.

   b. A British warship.

   c. Benedict Arnold's nickname for George Washington.

   d. None of the above.

3 What was the result of the Battle of Valcour Island?

   a. After a grueling battle, the Americans were forced to sail away by night.

   b. The British captured Arnold's ship, the *Congress*.

   c. A small American force defeated a superior British fleet.

   d. None of the above.

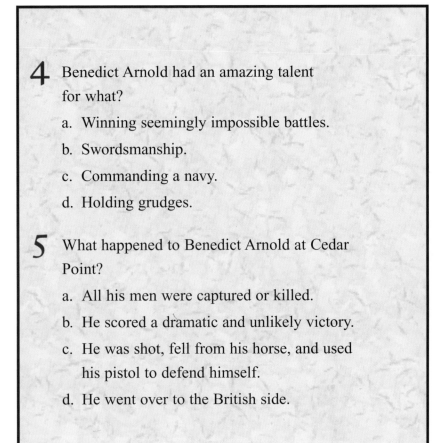

4 Benedict Arnold had an amazing talent
for what?

a. Winning seemingly impossible battles.

b. Swordsmanship.

c. Commanding a navy.

d. Holding grudges.

5 What happened to Benedict Arnold at Cedar
Point?

a. All his men were captured or killed.

b. He scored a dramatic and unlikely victory.

c. He was shot, fell from his horse, and used
his pistol to defend himself.

d. He went over to the British side.

ANSWERS: 1. c; 2. b; 3. a; 4. d; 5. c

The Battles of Saratoga

As the Americans prepared for battle, Congress began to reassess the officers in charge of the Continental Army in the north. Believing that someone should be held responsible for losing Ticonderoga, Congress dismissed Philip Schuyler as the commander of the northern army and replaced him with Horatio Gates.

The Congress also discussed what to do about Arnold. His supporters regarded him as a hero. His detractors doubted his commitment to the cause. After a good deal of argument, Congress decided not only to deny Arnold's request that his seniority be restored, but it also voted to accept his resignation. No one bothered to tell Arnold about the decision, however.

In August 1777, Arnold was at the American headquarters on the Hudson when Gates arrived to take over for Schuyler. Immediately, the army's officers began to argue, since some favored Schuyler and some favored Gates. Although Arnold was once friendly with both, he was now firmly in Schuyler's camp, which did not please his new commander.

Gates's northern army planned to confront the British troops along the Hudson River near the town of Saratoga. Marching north, they set up camp on a high cliff called Bemis's Heights. The British, led by General John Burgoyne, had established a camp nearby at the farm of John Freeman, an American who remained loyal to the British. For about a week, each army stayed put, leaving the soldiers anxious, fearing the other side would attack any minute.

Finally, on the morning of September 19, the American troops learned that the British army was heading toward them. By noon, a full-fledged battle had begun. For four hours, the bloody fight continued, with one side, then the other, taking the advantage. Arnold sent for reinforcements, but Gates refused his request. At nightfall, the two armies pulled back, ending what is now known as the Battle of Bemis's Heights.

Arnold wanted to fight the next day, despite a heavy fog. Instead, days passed with neither side making a move. An increasingly nervous Arnold learned that Gates had declared that, in the future, a corps of sharpshooters under Arnold's command would take orders only from Gates himself. Arnold was furious and insulted. He stormed into Gates's quarters and demanded an explanation.

During their argument, Gates informed Arnold that Congress had accepted his resignation. Stunned, Arnold said that he was leaving camp to take up the matter with Congress personally. Happy to see Arnold so upset, Gates encouraged him to go, since another major general, Benjamin Lincoln, was on his way to replace Arnold. According to a junior officer, "high

The Death of Jane McCrea

As the Continental Army prepared to fight the British forces led by General John Burgoyne near Saratoga, New York, it faced a difficult problem. The army desperately needed to recruit more men to join the fight as militiamen. But many New Yorkers did not want to get involved, fearing what might happen to them and their families if they openly defied Burgoyne's powerful fighting force.

In June 1777, the tragic death of a young woman changed their thinking. The woman was Jane McCrea, the fiancée of one of Burgoyne's aides. She was living with a loyalist friend, known to history only as Mrs. McNeil. McCrea's brother, an American militia officer, disapproved of her living situation. He sent a group of American militiamen to McNeil's house to bring McCrea to Albany, where he could keep an eye on her.

As the militiamen drew near, they attracted the attention of a group of British-allied Indians. The Indians reached the house first and captured McCrea and McNeil. They probably thought Burgoyne would reward them for the two captives. As the Indians raced toward Burgoyne's camp, the Americans chased after them, firing their guns. McNeil reached the camp safely, but McCrea was not so lucky. While aiming at the Indians, the Americans accidentally shot her three times. After she died, one of her captors, a Wyandot Indian named Panther, scalped her.

McCrea's death horrified Americans throughout the United States. Most assumed Panther had murdered her. Americans were already worried about Indian attacks, but McCrea's story made them more afraid than ever. American officers happily played on their fears, hoping to draw neutral New Yorkers into the militia. Benedict Arnold, for instance, wrote a fiery condemnation of the Indian attacks. The strategy worked. Hearing about McCrea's fate inspired thousands of men in New York and New England to sign up to fight on the American side.

The myth of Jane McCrea's death outlived the American Revolution, largely because of an 1804 painting by John Vanderlyn. The painting shows McCrea, still very much alive, set upon by two menacing Indian men who are preparing to scalp her. Very popular throughout the nineteenth century, Vanderlyn's painting helped spread the stereotype of Indian men as evil savages, eager to murder innocent white women in the most brutal ways imaginable.

words and gross language ensued, and Arnold retired in a rage."[8]

THE BATTLE OF FREEMAN'S FARM

Despite what Arnold said to Gates, he did not really want to leave the battlefield. He was eager to lead his troops and confident that they could beat the British force, who had sustained heavy casualties in the earlier battle. When Lincoln arrived, he sympathized with Arnold. He and his officers encouraged Arnold to stay. Still, Gates made it clear that Arnold was to keep away from the frontlines.

On October 7, Arnold learned that the long-awaited battle had begun in a wheat field near Freeman's Farm. After an hour of listening to the sound of gunfire, he could not take it anymore. Arnold mounted his horse and raced into the battlefield, waving his sword over his head. His men followed him into a clearing, where they charged the British again and again.

In the heat of the fray, Arnold's horse fell to the ground and rolled over his body. Pinned under the animal, his leg was broken in several places. Soldiers rushed to free him and carried him back to Bemis's Heights. In the field hospital there, Arnold begged the

In the heated battle near Freeman's Farm, Arnold was wounded when his horse fell.

medics not to amputate his leg, even though he was in horrible pain.

The following day, as the sun rose, Arnold learned that Burgoyne's army was in retreat, with the Americans in fast pursuit. Still in agony, he was moved to a hospital in Albany. While there, he received more welcome news: Near Saratoga, Burgoyne had been forced to surrender his entire army.

QUESTIONING THE CAUSE

The defeat of Burgoyne was a great victory for the northern army. However, the main army under Washington was having far less success. In September, it had failed to stall a British invasion of Philadelphia, forcing Congress to flee from the Continental capital.

Following his victory at Saratoga, Gates and his supporters began a campaign calling for Gates to replace Washington as commander-in-chief of the Continental Army. Naturally, Washington was annoyed by Gates's power grab. Knowing that Arnold was not friendly with Gates, Washington happily promoted Arnold as the real hero of Saratoga. In recognition of his service, Washington gave Arnold a set of French epaulets, fringed ornaments worn on the shoulder of a military uniform. Arnold treasured this gift.

Even with Washington's support, Arnold knew that he would not be seeing another battlefield anytime soon. His leg was not healing well, and he was in constant pain. When Arnold was finally released from the hospital, he returned to Connecticut to visit his family. On May 4, 1778, he arrived in New Haven. Still hobbling on crutches, Arnold was hailed as a hero during a celebration held on the village green.

Following the Battles of Saratoga, British General John Burgoyne was forced to surrender.

A few weeks later, Arnold traveled to Valley Forge, Pennsylvania, where Washington's troops had established their winter camps. Sick, hungry, and cold, about one-fourth of the men did not survive the winter. But by the time Arnold rode into camp, warmer weather and news of the Saratoga victory had encouraged the survivors, who were busily preparing for their spring campaign. Amidst the cheers of the soldiers, Arnold was enthusiastically welcomed by Washington himself.

Another man might have felt gratified by the warm reception. But for Arnold any recognition he received was outweighed by previous humiliations, whether real or imagined. While recuperating from his injuries, Arnold had had plenty of time to stew about various slights from other officers and members of Congress. More than ever, he came to wonder whether the American cause was worth all his hard work and sacrifice.

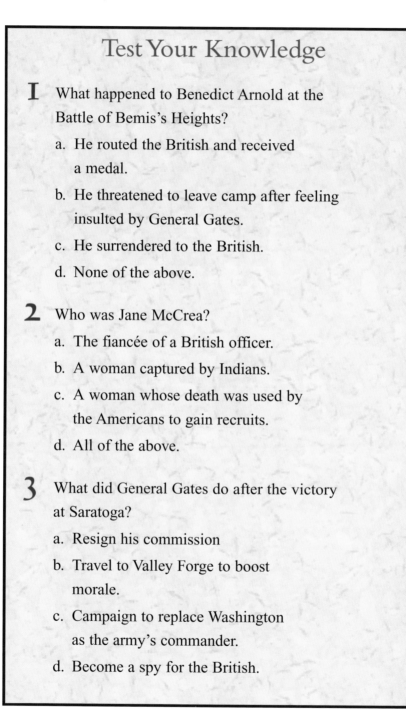

Test Your Knowledge

1 What happened to Benedict Arnold at the Battle of Bemis's Heights?

   a. He routed the British and received a medal.

   b. He threatened to leave camp after feeling insulted by General Gates.

   c. He surrendered to the British.

   d. None of the above.

2 Who was Jane McCrea?

   a. The fiancée of a British officer.

   b. A woman captured by Indians.

   c. A woman whose death was used by the Americans to gain recruits.

   d. All of the above.

3 What did General Gates do after the victory at Saratoga?

   a. Resign his commission

   b. Travel to Valley Forge to boost morale.

   c. Campaign to replace Washington as the army's commander.

   d. Become a spy for the British.

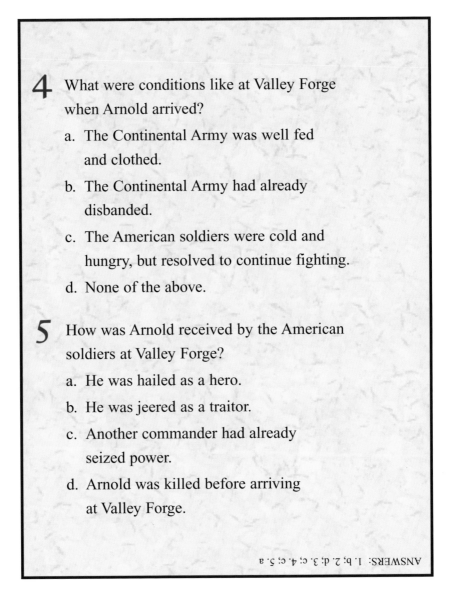

4 What were conditions like at Valley Forge when Arnold arrived?

   a. The Continental Army was well fed and clothed.

   b. The Continental Army had already disbanded.

   c. The American soldiers were cold and hungry, but resolved to continue fighting.

   d. None of the above.

5 How was Arnold received by the American soldiers at Valley Forge?

   a. He was hailed as a hero.

   b. He was jeered as a traitor.

   c. Another commander had already seized power.

   d. Arnold was killed before arriving at Valley Forge.

ANSWERS: 1. b; 2. d; 3. c; 4. c; 5. a

A General in Philadelphia

George Washington could not send Benedict Arnold into battle because of his injuries. Instead, he sent him to Philadelphia. In June 1778, the American army had regained control of the city from its British occupiers. Appointed Philadelphia's military governor, Arnold was charged with maintaining order there.

The job was not easy. A large number of Philadelphians were still loyal to the British crown. Although thousands of loyalists left the city with the British, many remained. Helping the loyalists and the rebels coexist in the city was a difficult task.

Even more challenging was negotiating Philadelphia's heated political life. In the building now known as Independence Hall, two law-making bodies met—the Continental Congress, which ruled all 13 states, and the Pennsylvania Council, which made laws for the state of Pennsylvania. The two groups fought constantly. As military governor of Philadelphia, Arnold often found himself in the middle of their conflicts.

Arnold disliked his job, but he loved living in Philadelphia. After a few years in the army, he was happy to indulge in the luxuries the large, sophisticated city could provide. Arnold moved into a stately mansion and invited his sister Hannah to join him. There, as host and hostess, they held elegant dinners and parties, offering guests the finest food and wine. Arnold invited not only congressmen and other politicians, but also members of Philadelphia's high society. Some of these guests were from families still loyal to Britain.

Arnold's house and parties were expensive. But he was willing to do whatever was necessary to come up with the cash to pay for them. Arnold developed a series of secret schemes to make money. While they were not strictly illegal, they were unethical, since they relied on making money at the expense of the war effort.

Soon after arriving in Philadelphia, Arnold invested in a few ships owned by Robert Shewell, who was thought to be a loyalist. Arnold gave Shewell a pass to transport goods from Philadelphia to Connecticut aboard the *Charming Nancy,* even though Arnold did not have the authority to do so. Arnold made another dubious arrangement with business partner John Livingston. Arnold learned that there was a French fleet off the coast of New York that would likely soon help the Americans reclaim that city, which had been captured by the British in late 1776. Arnold told Livingston to buy up all the goods he could in New York and stash them away. When the Continental Army took back the city, Arnold and Livingston could sell them for a high profit.

A NEW ENEMY

While climbing Philadelphia's social ladder, Arnold became smitten with an 18-year-old woman named

In Philadelphia, Arnold fell in love with 18-year-old
Peggy Shippen, the daughter of prominent Chief Justice
Edward Shippen (shown here).

Margaret Shippen, known as Peggy. Some Philadelphians thought his attentions toward Peggy were not
appropriate, since her family was sympathetic to the
British. Among them was Joseph Reed, a prominent

Philadelphia lawyer. Reed was already outraged by Arnold's high living. He thought the governor's fancy parties were a scandal, considering how many Americans were suffering because of the war.

Courting Peggy

Soon after Benedict Arnold arrived in Philadelphia, he became a fixture at society functions. Arnold tried hard to dazzle the city's elite with his reputation as a war hero. But he was particularly eager to make a good impression on Peggy Shippen—a lovely young woman from one of Philadelphia's most prominent families.

Peggy was well known in society circles. While the British occupied Philadelphia, she often went to parties hosted by British army officers. Many Philadelphians frowned on young women like Peggy, who consorted with the enemy.

But this mattered little to Arnold. He fell madly in love with Peggy and did everything he could to earn her affection. The courtship was whispered about all over Philadelphia. A letter written by a friend of Peggy's sister captures the city's fascination from the unlikely romance between Arnold and a society beauty 20 years his junior: "They say she intends to surrender soon. I thought the fort would not hold out long.

In October 1778, Reed saw a chance to discredit Arnold. Probably prompted by Reed, a militia sergeant levied an official complaint against Arnold. Arnold's aide, David Franks, had ordered the sergeant to find

Well, after all, there is nothing like perseverance and a regular attack."

Still, Arnold knew he had to do more than win Peggy's heart. He had to also persuade her family that he would make a suitable husband, which meant that he had to amass enough money to maintain their daughter's lavish lifestyle.

Indeed, when Peggy finally consented to marry Arnold, her family asked for a hefty dowry. Traditionally, a dowry was money or property that a husband gave a wife before her wedding. At first, Arnold worried that he would never be able to afford to marry Peggy, even with all his shady financial dealings. But he was eventually able to scrape together some £16,000, which he spent on a grand stone mansion called Mount Pleasant. Once Arnold signed the estate over to Peggy, the Shippens allowed the couple to announce their wedding date.

Source: Clare Brandt, *The Man in the Mirror: A Life of Benedict Arnold* (New York: Random House, 1994), 156.

him a barber. The sergeant's father wrote an angry note to Arnold. He was annoyed that Franks would waste the young soldier's time on a trivial personal errand. Arnold insisted Franks had done nothing wrong, blithely dismissing the criticism.

Later in the same month, Arnold learned that the *Charming Nancy* was almost destroyed in a British attack. Having secretly invested in the ship, Arnold was desperate to save its cargo. He sent army wagons to New York to pick up the goods there and bring them back to Pennsylvania. Although he promised to pay the wagon train's expenses, Arnold was clearly using army equipment for his personal business. At the same time, Arnold issued an illegal pass, hoping to enable a young woman named Hannah Levy to get into British-held New York. He had asked Levy to smuggle a letter into the city. (It was probably addressed to someone involved in one of his questionable business deals.) American troops, however, sent Levy back to Philadelphia before she could reach New York.

Unknown to Arnold, Reed had learned of Arnold's many schemes, including his appropriation of the army wagons and issuing of the illegal pass to Levy. Having been appointed to serve as president of the

Pennsylvania Council, Reed was more than willing to use his power and influence to further his personal vendetta against Arnold. At his urging, Congress appointed a committee to investigate the matter.

FACING COURT-MARTIAL

In early February 1779, Arnold learned of Reed's charges. There were eight in all. Two were fairly frivolous, but six were serious. Although Arnold was probably guilty of the important charges, Arnold never considered admitting the truth. He denied all the charges and attacked Reed and his allies. Arnold called them "a set of unprincipled, malicious scoundrels who have prostituted their honor and truth for the purpose of gratifying their private resentment against an innocent person."[9]

Nevertheless, the charges gnawed at Arnold. He was especially afraid of losing Peggy, who had agreed to marry him. But she remained completely loyal to him throughout the entire ordeal. Her family also rallied to support Arnold. When Reed asked the Pennsylvania Council to decide whether Arnold should remain Philadelphia's military governor, the only vote in Arnold's favor was cast by one of Peggy's relatives.

On April 4, four days before his wedding, Arnold found out that Congress had decided to subject him to a court-martial—a trial in a military court. It had found enough evidence to try him on four of the eight charges raised by Reed. While Arnold was on his honeymoon, he brooded. He had long felt that his fellow Americans were not paying him the respect he deserved. As the trial neared, Arnold's paranoia deepened, convincing him that his countrymen had betrayed him. In his eyes, it was only reasonable that he do the same to them.

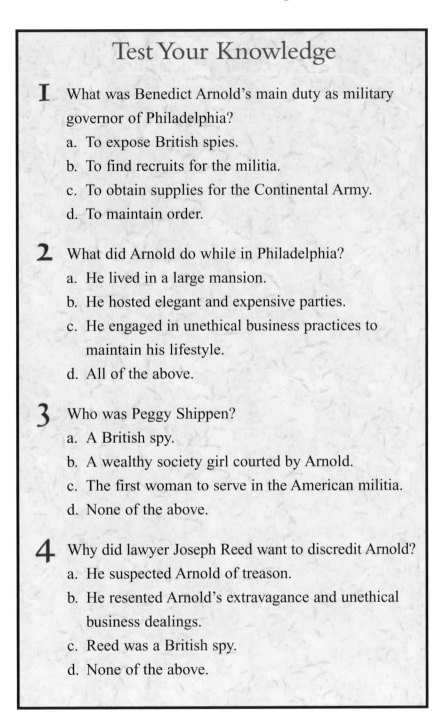

Test Your Knowledge

1 What was Benedict Arnold's main duty as military governor of Philadelphia?

  a. To expose British spies.

  b. To find recruits for the militia.

  c. To obtain supplies for the Continental Army.

  d. To maintain order.

2 What did Arnold do while in Philadelphia?

  a. He lived in a large mansion.

  b. He hosted elegant and expensive parties.

  c. He engaged in unethical business practices to maintain his lifestyle.

  d. All of the above.

3 Who was Peggy Shippen?

  a. A British spy.

  b. A wealthy society girl courted by Arnold.

  c. The first woman to serve in the American militia.

  d. None of the above.

4 Why did lawyer Joseph Reed want to discredit Arnold?

  a. He suspected Arnold of treason.

  b. He resented Arnold's extravagance and unethical business dealings.

  c. Reed was a British spy.

  d. None of the above.

5 How did Arnold answer Reed's charges against him?

a. He denied all charges and attacked Reed.

b. He confessed and was hauled away in irons.

c. He fled Philadelphia in shame.

d. None of the above.

ANSWERS: 1. d; 2. d; 3. b; 4. b; 5. a

A Traitor to the Cause

By early May 1779, Benedict Arnold had made his decision. He sent a letter to General Henry Clinton, the commander-in-chief of the British army. In it, he offered his services to the enemy.

In all likelihood, he had already shared his plans with his young wife Peggy. As she always did, Peggy supported

Arnold's choice. She even enlisted the help of John André, a handsome young aide to Clinton she had met during the British occupation of Philadelphia.

A few days after making his offer, Arnold had his first meeting with André, who assured Arnold that the British were still fully committed to winning the war. His words comforted Arnold. Now that he had joined the British side, he wanted to be sure that they would be victorious.

André was less encouraging about another of Arnold's concerns. Continually strapped for money, Arnold wanted to know exactly how much England was willing to pay him for his treachery. André promised him that he would receive ample compensation, but he was unwilling to give a precise amount.

Arnold enthusiastically plunged into his new role as a spy for the British. First, he visited the headquarters of the Continental Army and tried to regain the favor of George Washington. The charges against Arnold bothered Washington, but he was willing to give his old friend the benefit of the doubt. Welcomed back into Washington's inner circle, the deceitful Arnold gathered intelligence about the general's military plans that he could pass on to the British.

TROUBLES ON THE HUDSON

On June 1, 1779, Arnold turned his attention to his court-martial. But after its first day, the trial was postponed. The Continental Army had learned that Clinton's troops had captured two forts along the Hudson. Washington's army prepared to march north to take back the forts, and the court-martial was placed on hold.

In the meantime, Arnold kept busy. He worked hard to raise all the money he could before his treason was revealed. In addition to trying to sell his house in New Haven, he pressured Congress to reimburse expenses he had paid out of pocket in Philadelphia and during the Canadian campaign. But with the court-martial charges still standing against him, Congress was not eager to settle his accounts.

Arnold also devoted plenty of time to sharing intelligence with the British. He met with André several times and sent him numerous letters, filled with information. But still he heard nothing from the British about how much they would pay him. At last, André contacted Arnold, explaining that the British would not discuss money until he had provided intelligence that gave them a "real advantage."[10]

Arnold was furious, but his mood grew even worse after his court-martial reconvened in December. The following month, Arnold was found guilty of only one of the four charges against him. Yet his single conviction furthered his belief that the American army was persecuting him.

The Court-Martial of Benedict Arnold

Looking proud and confident, Benedict Arnold entered a tavern in Morristown, New Jersey, on December 23, 1779. He was dressed in his uniform, wearing gold epaulets that General George Washington had given to him to honor his distinguished military service.

That day was the first of Arnold's court-martial. For months, Arnold had prepared his defense, which he delivered himself. Arnold was probably guilty of all four charges against him. But, being a practiced liar, he had little trouble proclaiming his innocence, loudly and repeatedly. Arnold began by reminding the officers in the court of his military exploits during the American Revolution.

After this opening statement, Arnold carefully built a defense on each charge. He was especially effective in cross-examining witnesses delivering damaging testimony. Like a seasoned trial lawyer, he attacked his accusers,

TARGETING WEST POINT

By early 1780, it was clear what the British most wanted from Arnold. The British army had its eye on West Point, an American post on the Hudson. If the British took over the fort there, they would control the river, an important American supply route. The British

flustering them so much that it was nearly impossible for those watching to figure out who was telling the truth.

On January 26, 1780, the day the verdict was announced, Arnold walked into the courtroom with his head held high. He was sure that he would be found not guilty of all counts. Arnold was almost right. The court acquitted him of three charges, but found him guilty of granting an illegal pass to the *Charming Nancy,* a ship owned by a business partner. The sentence was light: Arnold would receive an official reprimand from Washington.

Perhaps because Washington felt uncomfortable dressing down his old friend, he took more than two months to write the reprimand. Nevertheless, Arnold was infuriated by Washington's reprimand. He became even more determined to get his revenge on the Continental Army and its commander-in-chief.

The fort at West Point, located on the Hudson River, protected a critical American shipping route. A British victory there, many believed, would end the war.

thought that seizing West Point would deal the death blow to the American army and end the war with a British victory.

Arnold sent an offer to General Clinton. He said that he could deliver West Point in exchange for £10,000 in cash and the command of a battalion of British soldiers. To further persuade Clinton, Arnold visited the fort and then sent the general a detailed plan for a British attack.

But once again, Clinton offered Arnold nothing but vague reassurances. Arnold received a letter from André on July 13, 1780. Dodging Arnold's request for £10,000, he explained that Arnold would have to "rely on [Clinton's] promise that upon effectual cooperation you shall experience the full measure of the national obligation." [11]

Arnold was unwilling to rely on promises. He angrily increased his demands to three payments— £10,000 paid upfront, £500 more paid each year, and a £20,000 bonus paid when he delivered West Point to the British.

Arnold's letter to André left out a crucial detail—he did not have any control over West Point. Arnold had let Washington know that he wanted command over the post, but Washington had not yet taken any action. To make his case to the general, Arnold traveled to Washington's headquarters on the Hudson at the end of

July. There, he finally persuaded Washington to name him the new commander of West Point. Arriving at the fort on August 5, 1780, Arnold pretended that he wanted to make repairs to the fort and to obtain desperately needed supplies. Privately, Arnold was plotting against the men he commanded. He delivered to the British reports about the fort's manpower and arms, all designed to help them seize it.

Many of the officers at West Point were old friends of Arnold's. Some had fought side by side with him at Quebec or Saratoga. But Arnold seemed to have little concern for what would happen to them if his plot succeeded. As he was well aware, if the British took West Point, his former comrades would likely be taken prisoner or killed.

THE PLOT UNRAVELS

Arnold did care about the safety of Peggy and their infant son Edward. He made plans for them to join him at Robinson House, a mansion near West Point where Arnold had established his headquarters.

Arnold carefully prepared for Peggy's arrival, arranging a delivery of fresh milk and meat and ordering a new feather bed. Arnold was frantic to

Arnold arranged for Peggy and their infant son, Edward, to join him at his headquarters near West Point.

obtain a guarantee of cash from the British. Finally, on August 24, he received a response from André. Clinton was offering Arnold a flat £20,000 if he turned West Point over to the British. But if the plot failed, he would get nothing.

Always sensitive to the smallest slight, Arnold went into a rage. To him, Clinton's offer was a grievous insult. He sent off a note to André, insisting on a face-to-face meeting at Robinson House. From then on, Arnold determined, he, not Clinton, would dictate the terms of his deal with the British.

The idea of the meeting, though, was foolhardy and dangerous. If André was caught in American territory, he would be executed as a spy. Arnold did not care. All that mattered to him was that Clinton and André start playing by his rules.

After several failed attempts to meet André, Arnold finally came up with a workable plan. He enlisted the help of Joshua Smith, a wealthy landowner who lived nearby. In awe of Arnold's military career, Smith was eager to do anything Arnold told him to do. Ignorant of Arnold's treason, Smith agreed to take a boat to pick up André from the *Vulture,* a British ship anchored in Haverstraw Bay. Smith then brought him to a point on the shore where Arnold was waiting.

In the early hours of September 22, Arnold had his meeting with André. It proved the undoing of them

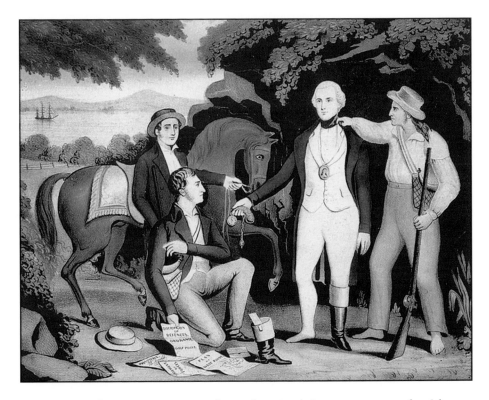

On September 23, 1780, Major John André was captured with documents that revealed that Arnold was a spy.

both. The next morning, André was captured while carrying documents that revealed that Arnold was a British spy. Hearing of André's fate, Arnold fled Robinson House, safely escaping to the *Vulture,* which carried him off to New York and a new life.

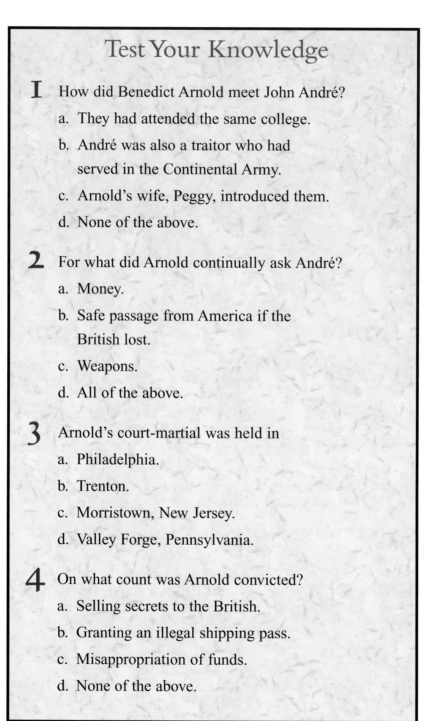

Test Your Knowledge

I How did Benedict Arnold meet John André?

   a. They had attended the same college.

   b. André was also a traitor who had served in the Continental Army.

   c. Arnold's wife, Peggy, introduced them.

   d. None of the above.

2 For what did Arnold continually ask André?

   a. Money.

   b. Safe passage from America if the British lost.

   c. Weapons.

   d. All of the above.

3 Arnold's court-martial was held in

   a. Philadelphia.

   b. Trenton.

   c. Morristown, New Jersey.

   d. Valley Forge, Pennsylvania.

4 On what count was Arnold convicted?

   a. Selling secrets to the British.

   b. Granting an illegal shipping pass.

   c. Misappropriation of funds.

   d. None of the above.

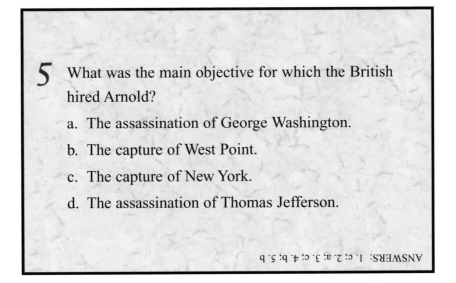

5 What was the main objective for which the British hired Arnold?

a. The assassination of George Washington.

b. The capture of West Point.

c. The capture of New York.

d. The assassination of Thomas Jefferson.

ANSWERS: 1. c; 2. a; 3. c; 4. b; 5. b

9

Fighting America

On the morning of September 26, 1780, Benedict Arnold arrived at British headquarters in New York. If he expected a warm welcome, he was surely disappointed. Largely because of his foolish demands for a face-to-face meeting with André, the British plot to seize West Point had fallen apart.

General Henry Clinton was very upset to lose West Point. He had been counting on the British capture of the fort, certain that the demoralized American army would quickly surrender. As a result, when Clinton met Arnold in New York, he did not see a brilliant military man who could help win the war. He saw an arrogant, selfish traitor who could not be trusted to make good on his promises.

Clinton had another reason to dislike Arnold. He blamed Arnold for André's capture by American troops. André was well liked by his fellow officers and was a personal favorite of Clinton's.

Arnold wrote a letter to George Washington, making a case for André's release. Washington ignored his reasoning and insisted that André be tried as a spy before a panel of officers. During the hearing, André confessed. Wanting to follow military law to the letter, Washington had no choice but to order his execution.

André's captors came to like and respect the charming young British officer while he was in their custody. Washington even sent food from his own table to André's prison cell every day. Many Americans were filled with awe by the dignity and bravery André displayed as he was marched to the gallows. Washington's aide, Alexander Hamilton, wrote, "in the midst of his enemies he died universally esteemed and universally regretted."[12] André's many British friends and colleagues also mourned him. Some said that in a just world, it would have been Arnold's neck, not André's, in the noose.

LOSING PEGGY

In the midst of this crisis, Arnold heard from his beloved wife Peggy. She had been given the choice between following her husband to New York or returning to her parents in Philadelphia. Peggy had decided to live with her family instead of Arnold.

The day Arnold discovered André had been captured, he fled to British territory, leaving Peggy at the American headquarters at Robinson House. Although in a panic, Peggy quickly made a plan to save herself. She destroyed every document she could find that implicated her in Arnold's treason. Then, still in her nightgown, she began to scream. The American officers in the house rushed to help her. Pretending to be hysterical, she clutched her infant son to her chest, shrieking that she knew that they were trying to kill him.

Peggy's theatrics earned the American officers' sympathy. They could not believe that such a young, beautiful, and sensitive woman could have known of Arnold's schemes. With Washington's consent, they escorted her safely into the arms of her loving family.

Cut off from his wife and family, Arnold was desperate to establish a respectable life in the British military. Clinton gave him the rank of brigadier general and the right to raise his own regiment, named the American Legion. But Arnold wanted more. He begged the British commander-in-chief for payment for his services as a spy. Clinton reluctantly offered him £6,000, far less than the £20,000 he would have received if he had turned West Point over to British forces.

Arnold then set about trying to build up both his regiment and his reputation in a series of public proclamations addressed to the people of America. In one, he offered good wages to any American soldier who joined the British army. In another, he desperately tried to explain why he had turned traitor. Arnold had previously claimed that his treason was proof that he was a real patriot, since America would be best served by remaining loyal to the British king.

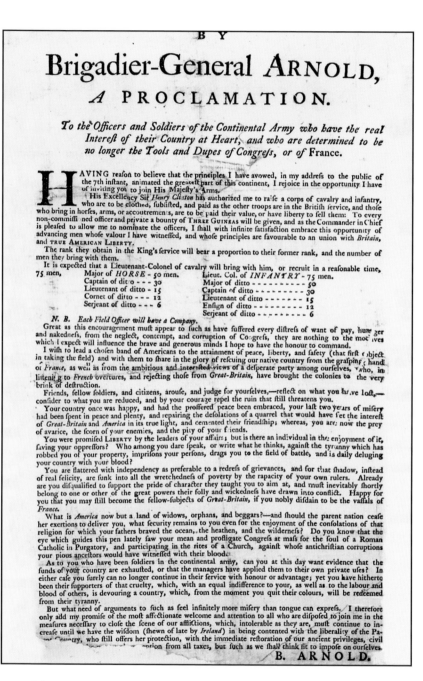

Arnold issued a series of public proclamations, urging American soldiers to join the British Army.

In his new proclamation, he added another justification. After the American victory at Saratoga, France, a Catholic nation, became the ally of the United States. Arnold claimed that this was proof of a Catholic plot to destroy America, whose citizens were mostly Protestants.

Few were convinced, especially after newspapers began publishing the details of Arnold's shady business deals. Most Americans believed that Arnold had turned traitor for one obvious reason—money. Throughout America, people held parades featuring effigies (dummies) dressed up to represent Arnold. When an effigy was set on fire as part of the festivities, crowds of patriots inevitably cheered.

The growing hatred of Arnold soon spread to Peggy, as well. Although her family continued to claim that she had been innocent of Arnold's scheming, the Pennsylvania Council decided to banish her from the state. With nowhere else to go, Peggy and her son moved to New York to join her husband, now the most hated man in America.

PROTECTING PORTSMOUTH

Against all evidence, Arnold still believed that he could

restore his reputation. He knew that the best place to do this was on the battlefield. A few weeks after Peggy's arrival, Arnold sailed off for Portsmouth, Virginia. Accompanied by a sizable fighting force, he was ordered to strengthen the British fort there. Clinton also told Arnold to destroy any American stores of ammunition he found along the way.

When Arnold reached the Virginia coast, he discovered that there were no American soldiers guarding the road to Richmond, the state's capital. Arnold decided to storm the town. His men marched into Richmond and set fire to its weapons stores along with many of its shops. Although it was hardly his most heroic moment, Arnold was happy once again to be in the thick of the fight.

A few days later, Arnold's men arrived at Portsmouth. As they began building up its fortifications, Arnold grew restless, desperate for a battle. By the middle of February, it began to look like he would get his wish. A British force, led by General Charles Cornwallis, had just suffered a terrible defeat in South Carolina. Cornwallis and his men were heading north to Portsmouth, with the American army chasing them. A French fleet also descended on the coast. It looked like Portsmouth would be the site of a major battle, until British ships defeated the French at sea. With this British victory, Portsmouth was again safe, foiling Arnold's chance to demonstrate to Clinton his worth in battle.

THE RAID ON NEW LONDON

In June 1781, Arnold returned to New York, still hoping for action. Finally, in September, he was ordered to set sail for New London, Connecticut, to stage a raid on the shipping town. Arnold knew it well. It was only about 12 miles from his childhood home.

Arnold had two targets. He needed to attack both New London and Fort Griswold, an American post across the Thames River from the town. He ordered a lieutenant colonel to lead the attack on the fort, while he took most of his troops into New London.

On September 6, Arnold's soldiers ran through the town's streets, setting fire to buildings and terrorizing the residents. Arnold's brutal raid was a success. The attack on Fort Griswold, however, turned into a bloody free-for-all. The British soldiers slaughtered most of the Americans there, continuing the killing even after the Americans had surrendered.

The Massacre at Fort Griswold

Hours into his assault on New London, Benedict Arnold rode his horse onto a high hill above the town. There, he put a spyglass to his eye and scanned across the Thames River until he could see Fort Griswold. He had sent a young lieutenant colonel, Edmond Eyre, to seize the American post with a force of 850 soldiers. He wanted Eyre's men to take control of the fort's guns and turn them on American ships sailing the river.

Getting his first good look at the fort, Arnold realized that he had miscalculated Griswold's defenses. The fort was much better armed than he had thought. Arnold fired off an order to Eyre to abandon the attack, and then rode down the hill to oversee the continuing attack on the town below.

Unknown to Arnold, this order never reached Eyre. For 40 minutes, his men struggled to storm the fort's walls amidst heavy fire. About 140 British soldiers were killed or wounded. Among the casualties were Eyre and his second in command.

Finally, the British troops made their way into the fort. They brutally attacked the Americans inside, who were outnumbered by at least four to one. Led by Lieutenant Colonel William Ledyard, the Americans, who included teenage boys and elderly men, were not equipped to defend themselves. When a British officer approached Ledyard, demanding to know who commanded the fort, Ledyard replied, "I did, sir, but you do now." Just as Ledyard made this declaration of surrender, British soldiers rushed toward him and stabbed him to death with bayonets.

The slaughter continued for several minutes before the surviving British officers could stop their men. In the end, 113 out of 140 of the Americans in Fort Griswold were dead or badly wounded. Americans were horrified by the news of the battle, which they called a massacre. Even the British questioned the conduct of the soldiers at Fort Griswold. Although Arnold was not present, many blamed him for what had had happened. His villainous reputation had made Arnold an easy scapegoat among the British, as well as the Americans.

Source: Willard Sterne Randall, *Benedict Arnold: Patriot and Traitor* (New York: William Morrow, 1990), 588.

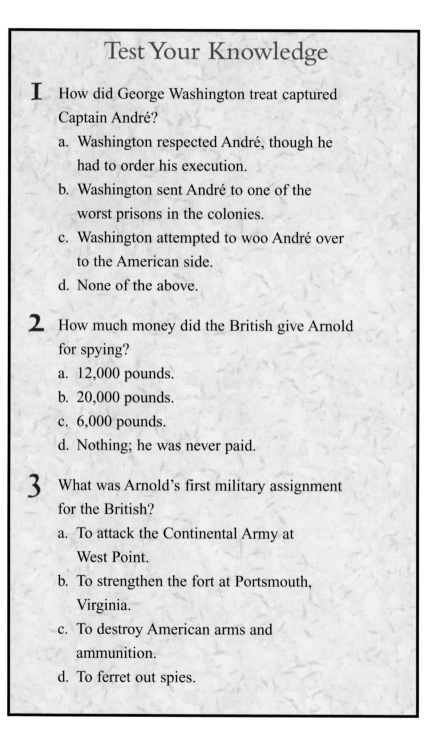

Test Your Knowledge

I How did George Washington treat captured
Captain André?

   a. Washington respected André, though he
had to order his execution.

   b. Washington sent André to one of the
worst prisons in the colonies.

   c. Washington attempted to woo André over
to the American side.

   d. None of the above.

2 How much money did the British give Arnold
for spying?

   a. 12,000 pounds.

   b. 20,000 pounds.

   c. 6,000 pounds.

   d. Nothing; he was never paid.

3 What was Arnold's first military assignment
for the British?

   a. To attack the Continental Army at
West Point.

   b. To strengthen the fort at Portsmouth,
Virginia.

   c. To destroy American arms and
ammunition.

   d. To ferret out spies.

4 What happened at Fort Griswold?

   a. Arnold restored his reputation as a gentleman-soldier.

   b. The British took the fort and massacred the Americans inside.

   c. The Americans successfully defended the fort against Arnold and Eyres.

   d. None of the above.

5 Most Americans blamed the outcome at Fort Griswold on

   a. The ill-equipped Continental Army.

   b. Lt. Colonel Eyres and his men.

   c. Benedict Arnold.

   d. George Washington.

ANSWERS: 1. a; 2. c; 3. b; 4. b; 5. c

In
Disgrace

After the raid on New London, Arnold hoped for still another opportunity to redeem himself in battle. He desperately wanted to go to Virginia, where General Cornwallis was engaged in a difficult campaign. But in late October 1781, alarming news reached British-held New York. In Yorktown, Virginia, Cornwallis had surrendered his army to the American forces led by George Washington.

Many saw the surrender as a fatal blow for the British. But Arnold refused to believe that the war was over. He pleaded with Clinton to allow him to travel to London. Arnold was sure he could convince the British government to stand firm and continue the fight.

In London, Arnold met with various political leaders, including King George III. He told them that if the British committed more money and more soldiers to fighting the rebel Americans, they were sure to win. The king supported Arnold's plan, but members of the British Parliament seemed uninterested in what he had to say. They voted to negotiate a peace treaty with the new United States. The American Revolution had ended, and Arnold found himself on the losing side.

Arnold tried to rebuild his life in London. But he soon discovered it would not be easy. The British public seemed to hate him almost at much as the American people. The British still loved John André and blamed Arnold for his death. As one popular poem declared, "Our troops by Arnold thoroughly were banged,/ And poor St. André was by Arnold hanged." [13]

The British government also showed their disdain for Arnold. After the war, he applied for compensation for his lost American property, but received nothing. Even worse, his brigadier general's pay was cut by two-thirds. The king awarded his wife Peggy £500 a year, but neglected to give Arnold any pension at all.

Desperate for money, Arnold scrambled to find a job, only to find no one wanted to hire a famous traitor. A potential employer at the British East India Company bluntly explained the situation to Arnold, "Although I am satisfied of the purity of your conduct, [most people] do not think so." [14]

A HOME IN NEW BRUNSWICK

Four years after arriving in England, Arnold found a job on a ship headed for New Brunswick. A province of Canada, New Brunswick was still claimed by the British. After England lost the war, many loyalists from the United States had flocked there. For Arnold, New Brunswick seemed like a good place for a fresh start.

Using the £6,000 he had received for spying, Arnold built a house and invested in numerous businesses, including a store, a lumberyard, and a shipyard.

Arnold found rebuilding his life to be difficult. Even outside the United States, he found few people willing to hire a famous traitor.

He also financed the construction of a new merchant ship, named the *Lord Sheffield*. After about a year, Arnold returned to England to bring back Peggy and his family. The Arnolds now had three small children— Edward, James, and Sophia.

In New Brunswick, Peggy tried to make the best of their situation. She decorated their house with elegant furniture and dishes she had brought from England. Soon, Arnold's sister Hannah and Arnold's teenage son Henry joined them. In September 1787, Peggy had a fourth child, George, adding still one more to their crowded household.

The Arnolds continued to be plagued by problems, both financial and personal. Arnold's businesses in New Brunswick failed, involving him a series of lawsuits with creditors and partners. While the people of the colony initially welcomed Arnold, they eventually began to turn on him. His history as traitor only reinforced their suspicions that Arnold was a greedy and dishonest man. The growing tensions exploded one night, when Arnold's neighbors burned him in effigy outside his own house while Peggy and the children looked on.

FINAL DAYS

After saving for the trip for a year, the Arnolds returned to England in late 1791. They tried to begin again in London, but their dire financial situation made it difficult. Their savings gone, they had to survive on Benedict's modest military salary and Peggy's small pension.

Arnold still held out hope that he could persuade the British government to compensate him for his lost property. He began appealing for help directly to William Pitt, the British prime minister. In one letter, he explained the desperateness of his situation: "[Since the war, I have] experienced the most unmerited and mortifying abuse not only from my own countrymen but from many persons in England . . . . I now find myself deprived of my fortune and rank, and so far from being able to provide for and educate a numerous family of six sons and one daughter, that is barely in my power to support them decently."[15] More than a year and half passed before Pitt responded. He granted an annual pension of £100 to each of Arnold and Peggy's four children, but nothing to Arnold himself.

In 1794, Arnold returned to the sea. Working on a merchant ship, he sailed to the West Indies, where he was taken captive by the French. Calling himself "Anderson" to conceal his identity, Arnold managed to escape to a British army ship, which hired him to oversee its provisions.

Dueling Lord Lauderdale

On May 31, 1792, James Maitland, the Earl of Lauderdale, stood up to speak before the House of Lords in the British Parliament. He began to attack the Duke of Rutland, accusing his political rival of apostasy, or abandoning his principals. Noting that the duke had just received an army command post, Lauderdale added, "if apostasy could justify promotion, [the duke] was the most fit person for that command, General Arnold alone excepted."

Everyone might have quickly forgotten Lauderdale's sarcastic jab at Arnold, if Arnold himself had let the matter rest. But by this point in his life, Arnold was so desperate to shore up his reputation that he became furious at the slightest insult. After hearing of Lauderdale's remarks, Arnold demanded that he apologize. Lauderdale did, but too halfheartedly for Arnold's taste. Arnold then wrote out his own apology, but Lauderdale refused to sign it.

Rather than let the matter drop, Arnold challenged Lauderdale to a duel. Even before the two met, pistols in hand, rumors were spreading through London, claiming that Lauderdale had killed Arnold. His wife Peggy had to turn away friends who came to console her, explaining that Arnold was still very much alive.

The duel took place on July 6. As the two men turned to face each other, Arnold fired his gun, but the bullet missed Lauderdale. Arnold steeled himself, waiting for Lauderdale to fire. But Lauderdale, insisting that he had no grudge against Arnold, refused to shoot. Lauderdale then gave Arnold another apology. This time, Arnold accepted.

London newspapers rushed to report on the duel. At least one claimed that Lauderdale had not apologized, perhaps hoping to keep the story alive. Yet, Arnold's gutsy challenge to Lauderdale seemed to have impressed some important Londoners. A few political leaders, including Prime Minister William Pitt, began to show Arnold a little more respect after his showdown with Lauderdale.

Source: Clare Brandt, *The Man in the Mirror: A Life of Benedict Arnold* (New York: Random House, 1994), 266.

Arnold returned to England about a year later, deeper than ever in debt. The army was slow in reimbursing him for the provisions he had purchased on its behalf. To make matters worse, he insisted on moving the family into a big house he could scarcely afford and borrowed even more money to invest in dubious financial schemes. Distraught over their debts, Peggy was plagued by depression and illness, although she was able to give birth to still another child, William, in 1798.

Arnold's health gradually began to fail. He had long suffered from gout, a painful medical condition that affects the joints. By the end of 1800, his legs were grossly swollen, and he found it more and more difficult to breathe. Arnold grew heartier after a stay in the country, but had a serious relapse the following summer. He died in his London home on June 14, 1801.

HERO AND VILLAIN

Eighteen months before Arnold's death, his former friend George Washington had passed away. The first president of the United States and one of the most revered figures of modern history, Washington was mourned the world over. Britain even showed its respect for the great American general and statesman by firing a grand salute from its fleet stationed in the English Channel.

In contrast, the world was largely silent on learning of Arnold's death. His obituaries were brief, suggesting that no one knew quite what to say about him. Even to this day, it is difficult to make sense of Arnold's life. If we look at only his final 22 years, Arnold appears to be a terrible human being, whose vanity, selfishness, and foolish arrogance came very close to destroying America's attempt to win its freedom.

But if we look at Arnold's military career before he committed treason, we get a very different picture. In these early years, Arnold displayed extraordinary courage and cunning as he fearlessly led his men into battle, earning him a reputation as one of the most talented generals in the Continental Army. It is one of the great contradictions of his life that, if Arnold had died from his leg injuries at Saratoga, he would be remembered today as a great revolutionary hero.

Test Your Knowledge

I How was Arnold treated as a citizen of London?
   a. He was hailed as a loyal servant of King George.
   b. He was reviled as a traitor, and blamed for André's death.
   c. He found it easy to find work as a private citizen.
   d. None of the above.

2 How did Arnold do as a businessman in New Brunswick?
   a. His businesses failed and he found himself fighting with creditors.
   b. His businesses succeeded and people forgot his reputation as a traitor.
   c. His businesses failed and he took his own life.
   d. None of the above.

3 What was the outcome of Arnold's duel with the Earl of Lauderdale?
   a. Arnold killed Lauderdale with the first shot.
   b. Arnold failed to show up for the duel.
   c. Arnold's bullet missed Lauderdale, and the Earl refused to shoot back.
   d. Arnold and Lauderdale killed each other.

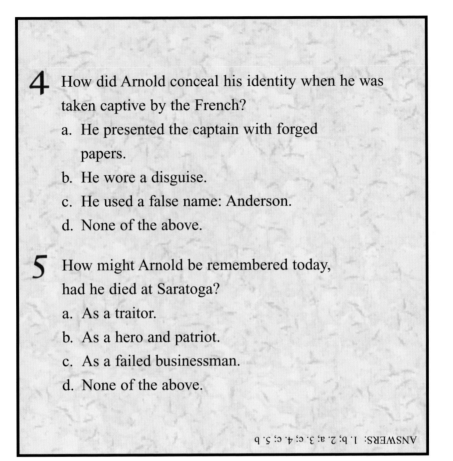

4 How did Arnold conceal his identity when he was taken captive by the French?

a. He presented the captain with forged papers.

b. He wore a disguise.

c. He used a false name: Anderson.

d. None of the above.

5 How might Arnold be remembered today, had he died at Saratoga?

a. As a traitor.

b. As a hero and patriot.

c. As a failed businessman.

d. None of the above.

ANSWERS: 1. b; 2. a; 3. c; 4. c; 5. b

1741 Benedict Arnold is born in Norwich, Connecticut, on January 14.

1752 Arnold attends school in Canterbury, Connecticut.

1755 Arnold is apprenticed to an apothecary after his family's bankruptcy.

1762 Arnold moves to New Haven, Connecticut.

1767 Arnold marries Margaret Mansfield.

1774 Arnold joins the Governor's Second Company of Foot Guards.

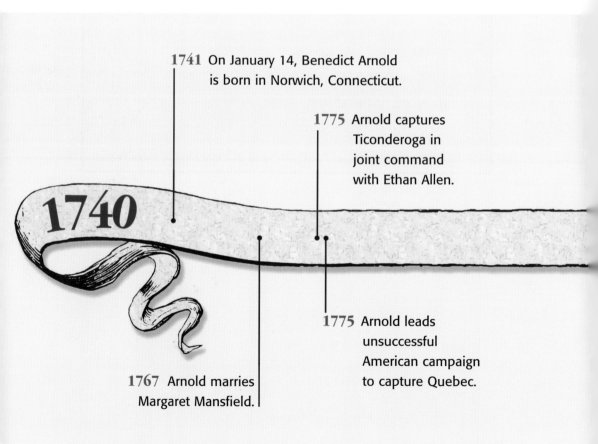

1741 On January 14, Benedict Arnold is born in Norwich, Connecticut.

1775 Arnold captures Ticonderoga in joint command with Ethan Allen.

1740

1767 Arnold marries Margaret Mansfield.

1775 Arnold leads unsuccessful American campaign to capture Quebec.

1775 Arnold joins the Massachusetts militia and captures Ticonderoga in joint command with Ethan Allen. Margaret Arnold dies in June. From September to December, Arnold leads unsuccessful American campaign to capture Quebec.

1776 Arnold fights British fleet at the Battle of Valcour Island.

1777 Arnold leads American militiamen against British soldiers in Connecticut, and distinguishes himself during the Battles of Saratoga.

1777 Arnold distinguishes himself during the Battles of Saratoga.

1779 Arnold approaches the British army with an offer to turn traitor.

1801 Arnold dies at his home in London at the age of 60 on June 14.

1805

1780 Arnold has secret meeting with British spy John André; flees to British-held New York after André is captured by American soldiers.

1778 Arnold is named military governor of Philadelphia, Pennsylvania.

1778 Arnold is named military governor of Philadelphia, Pennsylvania.

1779 Arnold is ordered to stand court-martial by Congress; marries Peggy Shippen. In May, he approaches the British army with an offer to turn traitor.

1780 In January, Arnold is found guilty of issuing an illegal pass at his court-martial. In August, he takes command of the fort at West Point on the Hudson River. He has secret meeting with British spy John André in September; flees to British-held New York after André is captured by American soldiers.

1781 Arnold leads attack on New London, Connecticut; blamed for the massacre of Americans at Fort Griswold.

1785 Arnold arrives in the British colony of New Brunswick.

1791 Arnold returns to London, England, with his family.

1801 On June 14, Arnold dies at his home in London at the age of 60.

Notes

CHAPTER 2
Struggling for Recognition
1. Willard Sterne Randall, *Benedict Arnold: Patriot and Traitor* (New York: William Morrow, 1990), 27.
2. Ibid.

CHAPTER 3
Attack on Ticonderoga
3. Clare Brandt, *The Man in the Mirror: A Life of Benedict Arnold* (New York: Random House, 1994), 34.

CHAPTER 4
Invading Canada
4. James Kirby Martin, *Benedict Arnold, Revolutionary Hero: An American Warrior Reconsidered* (New York: New York University Press, 1997), 102.

CHAPTER 5
On Land and on Sea
5. Brandt, *The Man in the Mirror,* 90.
6. Martin, *Benedict Arnold,* 263.

7. Brandt, *The Man in the Mirror,* 116.

CHAPTER 6
The Battles of Saratoga
8. Ibid., 136.

CHAPTER 7
A General in Philadelphia
9. Ibid., 170.

CHAPTER 8
A Traitor to the Cause
10. Ibid., 182.
11. Ibid., 195.

CHAPTER 9
Fighting America
12. Ibid., 229.

CHAPTER 10
In Disgrace
13. Brandt, *The Man in the Mirror,* 257.
14. Ibid., 259.
15. Ibid., 267.

Bibliography

Brandt, Clare. *The Man in the Mirror: A Life of Benedict Arnold.* New York: Random House, 1994.

Chambers, John Whiteclay II. *The Oxford Companion to American Military History.* New York: Oxford University Press, 1999.

Ethier, Eric. "The Making of a Traitor." *American History* 36, Issue 3 (August 2001): 22–31.

Koster, John. "Jane McCrea, Remembered as a Victim of American Indian Brutality, May Have Died Under Different Circumstances." *Military History* 17, Issue 2 (June 2000): 12.

Martin, James Kirby. *Benedict Arnold, Revolutionary Hero: An American Warrior Reconsidered.* New York: New York University Press, 1997.

Park, Edwards. "Could Canada Have Ever Been Our Fourteenth Colony?" *Smithsonian Institution* 18, Issue 9 (December 1987): 40–50.

Randall, Willard Sterne. *Benedict Arnold: Patriot and Traitor.* New York: William Morrow, 1990

———. "Why Benedict Arnold Did It." *American Heritage* 41, Issue 6 (September/October 1990): 60-72.

Fritz, Jean. *Traitor: The Case of Benedict Arnold.* New York: Putnam, 1997.

Gaines, Ann. *Benedict Arnold: Patriot or Traitor?* Berkeley Heights, N.J.: Enslow Publishers, 2001.

King, David C. *Benedict Arnold and the American Revolution.* Woodbridge, Conn.: Blackbirch Press, 1999.

———. *Saratoga.* Brookfield, CT: Twenty-First Century Books, 1998.

Lutz, Norma Jean. *Benedict Arnold: Traitor to the Cause.* Philadelphia: Chelsea House Publishers, 2000.

Strum, Richard M. *Fort Ticonderoga.* Philadelphia: Mason Crest Publishers, 2005.

WEBSITES

Benedict Arnold: The Making of a Traitor
www.americanhistory.about.com/library/prm/blbenedictarnold1.htm

Benedict Arnold: Revolutionary War Major General
www.benedictarnold.org

Fort Ticonderoga National Historic Landmark Museum
www.fort-ticonderoga.org/collections/objects/museum.htm

Historic Valley Forge
www.ushistory.org/valleyforge/served/arnold.html

Saratoga National Historic Park
www.nps.gov/sara

Second Company Governor's Foot Guard
www.footguard.org

Stories of Spies and Letters: The Infamous Benedict Arnold
www.si.umich.edu/spies/stories-arnold-1.html

Valcour Bay Research Project
www.historiclakes.org/vbrp/vbr1a.htm

Index

LIZ SONNEBORN is a writer living in Brooklyn, New York. A graduate of Swarthmore College, she has written more than 50 books for children and adults, including *The American West*, *A to Z of American Women in the Performing Arts*, and *The New York Public Library's Amazing Native American History*, winner of a 2000 Parent's Choice Award.